Mystical Theology: The Glosses by Thomas Gallus
and the Commentary of Robert Grosseteste on *De Mystica Theologia*

D1605492

DALLAS MEDIEVAL TEXTS AND TRANSLATIONS

EDITOR

Philipp W. Rosemann
(University of Dallas)

EDITORIAL BOARD

BOARD OF EDITORIAL ADVISERS

SPONSORED BY

UNIVERSITY OF DALLAS

DALLAS MEDIEVAL TEXTS AND TRANSLATIONS
3

Mystical Theology: The Glosses by Thomas Gallus and the Commentary of Robert Grosseteste on *De Mystica Theologia*

EDITION, TRANSLATION, AND INTRODUCTION
BY

James McEvoy
(National University of Ireland, Maynooth)

PEETERS
PARIS – LEUVEN – DUDLEY, MA
2003

Cover illustration: Gallus's glosses on the *Mystical Theology* in MS. *Munich, Bayerische Staatsbibliothek, Clm 7983*, fol. 126v. By kind permission of the Bayerische Staatsbibliothek, Munich.

Library of Congress Cataloging-in-Publication Data

Mystical theology: the glosses by Thomas Gallus and the Commentary of Robert
   Grosseteste on De mystica theologia / edition, translation, and introduction by James McEvoy.
      p. cm. -- (Dallas medieval texts and translations ; 3)
   Includes bibliographical references (p.).
   ISBN 90-429-1310-X (alk. paper)
      1. Pseudo-Dionysius, the Areopagite. De mystica theologia. 2. Mysticism--Early works
   to 1800. I. McEvoy, J. J. II. Thomas, Gallus, d. 1246. Exposicio Vercellensis. English &
   Latin. III. Grosseteste, Robert, 1175?-1253. Commentary De mystica theologia. English &
   Latin. IV. Pseudo-Dionysius, the Areopagite. De mystica theologia. English & Latin. V.
   Series.

   BR65.D63D4536 2003
   248.2'2--dc21

                                                                                2003045504

© 2003 – Peeters – Bondgenotenlaan 153 – B-3000 Leuven – Belgium.
ISBN 90-429-1310-X
D. 2003/0602/66

Mistica Theologia

Grosseteste's commentary on the *Mystical Theology* in MS. *Dublin, Trinity College 164*, fol. 263r. By kind permission of the Board of Trinity College Dublin.

Editor's Foreword

The Dallas Medieval Texts and Translations series pursues an ambitious goal: to build a library of medieval Latin texts, with English translations, from the period roughly between 500 and 1500, that will represent the whole breadth and variety of medieval civilization. Thus, the series will be open to all subjects and genres, ranging from poetry through philosophy, theology, and rhetoric to treatises on natural science. It will include, as well, medieval Latin versions of Arabic and Hebrew works. In the future, the publication of vernacular texts is a possibility. Placing these texts side by side, rather than dividing them in terms of the boundaries of contemporary academic disciplines, will, we hope, contribute to a better understanding of the complex coherence and interrelatedness of the many facets of medieval written culture.

In consultation with our distinguished board of editorial advisers, we have established principles that will guide the progress of the series. The primary purpose of the Dallas Medieval Texts and Translations is to render medieval Latin texts accessible in authoritative modern English translations; at the same time the series will strive to provide reliable texts in Latin where such are not yet available. The translations will therefore be established either on the basis of existing good critical editions (which we will not normally reprint) or, when necessary, on the basis of new editions. To enhance the accessibility of the texts to a wide academic public, including graduate students, the critical apparatus of the editions will be limited to important variants. Each volume will comprise scholarly introductions, notes, and annotated bibliographies.

Works published in the Dallas Medieval Texts and Translations series will be unexcerpted and unabridged. In the case of a work too long to appear in a single volume, we will start with the beginning of the work or publish integral parts of it, rather than creating a selection of discontinuous texts.

The third volume of the Dallas Medieval Texts and Translations brings together two closely related texts. Both are commentaries on the *Mystical Theology*, a treatise that has helped to shape Christian discourse upon God from the time of its composition, sometime in the early sixth century A.D., until the present day. The influence of the *Mystical Theology* on the tradition has been as profound and far-reaching as the identity of its author has remained mysterious. We still do not know who the Pseudo-Dionysius really was. Professor James McEvoy, the distinguished expert on the reception of the Dionysian writings in the West who is responsible for the present volume, speaks of two phases in the assimilation of Eastern mystical theology in the Latin Middle Ages.

The first of these phases occurred in Carolingian times, and was dominated by the figure of John Scottus Eriugena. The second phase was initiated, toward the middle of the twelfth century, by the two authors whose works are edited and translated in this book, Thomas Gallus and Robert Grosseteste. Since the two were not only co-workers in the field of mystical theology, but friends who exchanged their writings with each other, the publication of their commentaries in one volume is most appropriate. The significance of the treatises here published is best described in a sentence from Professor McEvoy's conclusion: "The entire later interpretation of the *Mystical Theology* was deflected into the path it actually followed through the combined influence of Thomas Gallus and Robert Grosseteste. These earliest Latin commentators provided the context within which not only the mystical theology of monastery and university but also the actual spiritual experience of countless souls was formed."

Thanks are due in the first place to the University of Dallas, whose financial support has made this series possible. Professor Glen Thurow, formerly Provost and Dean of Constantin College, believed in this project years before the first contributor submitted a manuscript. His successor, Professor Thomas Lindsay, has continued the University's generous assistance. Emmanuel and Paul Peeters enthusiastically embraced the idea for the Dallas Medieval Texts and Translations when we first discussed it with them in 1998. We are very pleased that our new series is associated with a publisher and printer of such great tradition and renown. Thanks are also due to the medievalists in the United States and abroad who have agreed to serve on our board of editorial advisers.

Philipp W. Rosemann
November, 2002

Table of Contents

Acknowledgments

A number of individuals and institutions deserve thanks for the help they have given me in the course of this work.

Hill Monastic Library supplied me with a microfilm copy of the Vienna manuscript of the *Exposicio* of Gallus. The *Bibliothèque municipale* at Besançon delivered a microfilm of the manuscript in their holding. The librarians of the Bavarian State Library, the Central Library of Zurich and the Jesuit Library, Milltown Park, Dublin, helped me with my inquiries. The National University of Ireland provided a generous grant in aid of publication. The librarians of the Russell Research Library at Maynooth lent their professional support to my endeavors. The editors of the Dallas series granted a subvention to help defray some of the expenses attached to research.

The Alexander von Humboldt-Stiftung (Bonn) made a grant for four months subsistence at Munich, where I was attached to the Institute of Philosophy of the university (1995). While I was at Munich Professor Werner Beierwaltes showed great interest in the research project and was helpful in innumerable ways. Dr. Catherine Kavanagh deserves my thanks for having conducted a computer-aided search for unidentified copies of the glosses of Thomas Gallus. The National University of Ireland, Maynooth, granted me research leave during the academic year 2001–2002 together with a research grant to cover the purchase of a computer, among other essential things. The Rector of the Down and Connor Diocesan Seminary (Belfast) generously provided me with an office while I was working on this book, and I received much hospitality from him and his colleagues. Ann Gleeson and Jacqui Mullally, executive assistants at the Faculty of Philosophy, NUI, Maynooth, smoothed the way very helpfully for the preparation of the volume. Mr. Hugh O'Neill gave much-appreciated help with the correction of the proofs.

Lastly I would like to thank my former student and friend, Philipp Rosemann, for agreeing to publish this book in the series of which he is the founder-editor, and also Dr. Michael Harrington, who along with him made valuable suggestions towards the improvement of its contents.

James McEvoy
Dean, Faculty of Philosophy
National University of Ireland, Maynooth
St. Patrick's Day 2002

PART I: THE *EXPOSICIO* OF THOMAS GALLUS

1. Introduction

Thomas Gallus, Abbot of Vercelli

Thomas Gallus *abbas Vercellensis* was born in France at a date unknown ("Gallus"; he was known in Italy as *Thomas Parisiensis*). He spent the first part of his life at the Augustinian Abbey of St. Victor at Paris, as a Canon Regular. He was a professor of theology at the University, lecturing at the Abbey, which had many members active in parishes and priories throughout the Paris area, catering chiefly for the needs of the large student body present in the city. In 1218–1219 Cardinal Guala Bicchieri, who was several times Papal Legate in France and England, appealed to the canons of St. Victor for help with the founding of an abbey and a hospital in his native Vercelli (N. Italy). Three members of the community, one of them Thomas, accompanied Guala back to Italy. He may well have been chosen for his combination of academic attainments and spirituality (qualities which Guala admired in the Victorine canons). Thomas became prior of the new foundation in 1224 and abbot the following year. He made a lengthy visit to England in 1238 but was back in Vercelli before the close of that year. In May 1243 he was forced to seek refuge at Ivrea, when deposed as abbot in the course of the bitter conflict between Guelphs and Ghibelines in the North of Italy. There are some indications that he may have been reinstated at Vercelli before his death, which took place in 1246. His remains lie in the church of the former abbey, San Andrea, which he helped to found. The inscription on his monumental tomb which was erased during the French Revolutionary period but is preserved in a copy, referred to him as *magister in Hierarchia*, recalling his fame as glossator of the writings of Pseudo-Dionysius. The latter is present in effigy on the monument, along with St. Andrew, the Blessed Virgin, and St. Catherine (patroness of philosophy).

Writings

Thomas wrote biblical commentaries as well as studies of the corpus of writings by the mysterious Greek-language theologian known as the Pseudo-Dionysius, who posed as the Areopagus council member, Denis, the convert of St. Paul (Acts 17). Throughout the Middle Ages he was accorded sub-apostolic authority. Commentaries of Thomas on

the Canticle (or Song of Songs) have survived, whereas his work on Isaiah is lost. He also compiled a biblical concordance, traces of the use of which can be found in his surviving writings. His compositions can be dated with an ease quite unusual for his era: in some instances the author entered completion dates by day, month and year; in others the time of composition can be established accurately on the basis of back-references he made to them in dated works. His authenticated writings relative to the Pseudo-Dionysian corpus can be dated quite accurately. They can be described as follows.[1]

Commentaries on the Pseudo-Dionysius

After many years of preparatory work Thomas composed glosses on all four works and two of the ten letters. He used the version by John Sarrazen, one of his predecessors among the Victorine canons. This work was completed by 1233. The glosses on the *Mystical Theology* (henceforth MT) which are edited in the present volume formed part of it.

Not content to leave the matter there he went on to write another digest, "extracting" the sense of the obscure author: the *Extractio* (1238). The work covers the four treatises and the Letter to Titus. It was very commonly considered in the Middle Ages to be a version alongside those of Eriugena, Sarrazen, and Grosseteste, even though Thomas was careful to make no such claim for it, for he had not enough Greek to translate, or to correct authoritatively the existing translations. The *versio princeps* of Hilduin, the abbot of St. Denis, knew but little circulation and survives in a single manuscript witness. The *Extractio* was the outcome of many years of close familiarity with the versions of Eriugena and Sarrazen, pursued until Thomas's own mind achieved a high degree of symbiosis with that of the Pseudo-Areopagite. It was, one might say, just the thing required by the busy university minds of his age, who were eager for doctrinal understanding but were largely untroubled by any kind of philological or antiquarian curiosity. The *Extractio* constitutes a literary genre all of its own. This "simplifying paraphrase" as one might term it, was to know a huge fortune after becoming an integral part of the standard university collection of translations and commentaries on the Pseudo-Dionysian writings.

Thomas followed up his success with a literal commentary in which each significant word or phrase is glossed and accompanied by an explanation. The *Explanacio* (as it came to be known) includes abundant reference to the Scriptures, as well as cross-references

---

[1] The best survey can be found in the art. "Thomas Gallus" by Jeanne Barbet, in *Dictionnaire de spiritualité ascétique et mystique*. For complete bibliographical details on this and other items cited in the footnotes, see Bibliography.

to other passages of the Pseudo-Dionysius. The only element of the *Explanacio* to have appeared in print is the *Mystical Theology*, composed at Vercelli towards 1241.[2]

To summarize: Thomas composed three separate sets of commentary on the writings of the Pseudo-Areopagite. The earliest (1233) is edited (in part — namely, the *Mystical Theology*) in this book, and will be given the title *Exposicio*. The second (1238) and best known was somewhat longer: the *Extractio*. The third and longest is known as the *Explanacio*; its various parts were finished between 1241 and 1243.

It is worth noting that in his prologue to the four sets of glosses he completed in 1233 Thomas acknowledged an unnamed colleague who had begun "to spin" the material Thomas set himself "to weave." In other words, like many scholars both before and after him, he did not set out from nothing. In the same context he expressed the hope that "from the oil-lees of a hard text" his own work had squeezed out "the oil of a fairly easy understanding" — at least for pure minds. Acquaintance with the *Exposicio* on the MT confirms that this modest boast was justified.

Authenticity of the Exposicio

Can we be quite sure of the grounds for attributing the *Exposicio* to Thomas? Since none of the manuscripts claims him as the author of the glosses resort must be had largely to internal evidence in support of his authorship. We know (as was said above) that Thomas wrote some sort of commentary on the MT ten years before he composed the *Explanacio*, for he tells us so himself. The earlier commentary in question cannot be the *Extractio*, for he completed that in 1238. Thus he can only be referring to the set of glosses which we have named *Exposicio* (because Thomas says, *exposui*, "I expounded").

But does internal analysis (for example of vocabulary and ideas) support this conclusion? On the basis of a detailed comparative examination of the glosses with the *Explanacio* (regarding their material interrelationship, exegetical approach, content and thought) the firm conclusion has been reached that the two works were written by the same man.[3] In the first place, both are based on the translation of Sarrazen, and even upon the same paragraph-division of that version as is found in the *Explanacio*. Both works were composed with the help of the same biblical concordance (the one compiled by Gallus himself). The most natural conclusion to be drawn from comparison between them is that the same author was responsible for both texts. The differences between the two writings are such as derive from their differing lengths.

---

[2] See *Thomas Gallus, Grand commentaire sur la Théologie mystique*, ed. Gabriel Théry, O.P. The glosses on five of the letters of Pseudo-Dionysius have been edited by J. Walsh (see Bibliography).

[3] The evidence is fully discussed in my 1999 article on Thomas Gallus.

Sources

Apart from the Bible and the writings of the Pseudo-Dionysius no source is actually referred to in the glosses. However, it requires only a little surface excavation to discover two. The first of these accounts for the notable and deliberate emphasis placed upon the Holy Trinity. The clue to this feature of the glosses is found when we turn to the *Explanacio*, which refers by name to only two figures of the past, *Iohannes Scotus* (for the *versio Dionysii*), and *prior Richardus de Santo Victore Parisiensi, in volumine quod dicitur Iustus meus*. This reference is to the celebrated *De Trinitate* which was Richard the Scotsman's masterpiece in speculative theology, and which was to exercise a notable influence within the schools. Gallus evidently admired it. His manner of referring to its author bespeaks both scholarly reverence and institutional pride.

The second indication of a source can be detected at the point where Thomas enunciates the Augustinian view that there is no ontological or causal intermediary between the soul and God. The sense of the formula *inter Deum et animam nihil cadit medium* is in fact found in many different places in St. Augustine's writings.[4] It was also conveyed to the Middle Ages by the treatise *De spiritu et anima*, which was compiled (by Alcher of Clairvaux?) in the mid-twelfth century.[5]

The Augustinian quality of Gallus's thought deserves some attention, in the light of his strenuous efforts to absorb the central message of MT. Like his contemporary, Robert Grosseteste, Gallus held firmly to the conviction that the beatific vision is unmediated by theophanies, being a "face to face" meeting. In this they were of course following the lead given by Hugh of St. Victor in his commentary on the *Celestial Hierarchy*. The result was a considerable, perhaps unconscious, attenuation of apophaticism.

Value

The firm attribution of the *Exposicio* to Thomas enhances its importance for the history of mystical thought quite considerably. This work turns out to have been the first fruits of his study of the *Corpus Dionysiacum* as a whole — a study which by the year 1233 already went back at least twenty years in his life. The *Exposicio* foreshadowed the renowned *Extractio* by the paraphrasing method it employed. The identification of the first of Thomas's commentaries on the Pseudo-Dionysian corpus, which may be looked upon as the prototype for the second and third, will enable scholars to observe the

---

[4] For instance, *De libero arbitrio* I.10.21; *De civitate Dei* XI.2; *De 83 quaestionibus*, qu. 54; *De vera religione* 55.113; *De Genesi liber imperfectus* 16.60; *Enarrationes in Psalmos* 118.18.4.
[5] It is printed *inter opera Augustini*, in PL 40: 779–832; see for instance ch. X, 785–86.

evolution of his interpretation. In this way the *Exposicio* will be restored to its true place of importance within the work of its author.

But that is not all. This set of glosses marks the beginnings of what I have elsewhere called the second Latin reception of the thought of the Pseudo-Dionysius, and of apophaticism in particular (the first Latin reception of the negative theology was the single-handed work of Scottus Eriugena).[6] The *Exposicio* has a broader significance than simply its role as the prototype of Gallus's own endeavors. The wider picture manifests its importance as the first Latin exegesis of the entire corpus of the Pseudo-Dionysius. The *Exposicio* belonged to the year 1233. In 1238 the *Extractio* followed. The *Explanacio* was completed by 1243. Between 1239 and 1242 Thomas's acquaintance, Robert Grosseteste, re-translated (as we shall see) the four works and added a detailed commentary. By the end of the 1240s Albert the Great had finished a major commentary on the same corpus.[7] By that time the Paris collection of Pseudo-Dionysian versions and glosses had been formed and put into circulation in the schools of the city. From all of this it now appears that the humble *Exposicio* turned out to be nothing less than the harbinger of an entire movement which was to continue up to 1500, and even beyond then.

Doctrine

To what extent are the glosses that make up the *Exposicio* doctrinally interesting and instructive? In the first place the interest which attaches to the *Extractio* and the *Explanacio*, both as commentaries on the MT and as witnesses to the personal religious or mystical thought of Thomas Gallus, can be found already present in the first general casting of Thomas's hermeneutical thought, the *Exposicio*. There Thomas puts forward his interpretation of the MT, in condensed form admittedly by comparison with his later works; on the other hand everything is somehow there from the start, and in particular the distinctive elements of the mystical vocabulary of Thomas are for the most part already present. At this point in our assessment of the value of the *Exposicio* a brief outline of the central tenets of Thomas's mystical thought will prove of help to the reader.

In his mystical interests Gallus continued a century-old in-house tradition at the Abbey of St. Victor. A hundred years before Thomas, Hugh had written a commentary on the *Celestial Hierarchy*, thus introducing the Pseudo-Dionysian works into the library,

---

[6] See Deirdre Carabine, *John Scottus Eriugena*, pp. 58–66.
[7] The composition of his commentary on the MT is placed by the best authority in 1250 and at Cologne: *Saint Albert le Grand: Commentaire de la Théologie Mystique de Denys, le Pseudo-Aréopagite*. Introduction, traduction, notes et index par Edouard-Henri Wéber, O.P (Paris: Cerf, 1993), p. 9.

and the school. Another canon, John Sarrazen, had produced his version of Dionysius there in 1166–1167. Prior Richard (the Scotsman already mentioned) in his turn had given distinctive impulses to mystical theology. Both Hugh and Richard were deeply influenced by St. Augustine, and so they gave a large place in their theology to love (*affectus, amor, benevolentia, caritas*). Thomas learned from both predecessors, but he also leaned towards St. Bernard. The Cistercian had chosen the *Canticum Canticorum* as the exegetical framework of his own doctrine of God, the *dilectus*, and soul, the *sponsa* or beloved. This he did through allegorization in the style of Origen. Thomas Gallus may be said to have drawn together all the impulses just mentioned and systematized them, in quasi-scholastic fashion. In particular, he developed an affective reading of the Areopagite, receiving the latter's apophatic thought into an Augustinian framework. At the same time Gallus followed the negative way with conviction and approved of its reversal of the conceptual understanding of God.

Thomas interpreted the MT in the light of the passage on the transcendental and cosmic nature of *eros* to be found in chapter 4 of the *Divine Names*. He advanced the view that when our knowledge of God runs out and the mind is forced to cease from all activity and enter the cloud of unknowing (as Moses did, according to MT ch. 1), love then takes over and, unaided by words, propositions, statements and concepts, is drawn beyond itself in *excessus*, that is to say, ecstasy or self-transcendence, towards union with the beloved, which is to say deification. Furthermore, love is itself a kind of knowledge. Thomas spoke of *nosse* as distinct from *scire*, that is to say, of knowledge by acquaintance, or knowledge by *experience* (the Bernardian term recurs under his pen): in other words, knowledge which transcends all the knowing gained through conceptual processes — and which is thereby actually truer and higher than the concept. This lofty knowledge fills the highest capacity of the soul, which is referred to by Thomas by means of those rather untranslatable signature-terms he repeatedly employs, such as *superintellectualis cognitio et affeccio* ("more-than-intellectual knowledge and affection"), or *affectus principalis* ("the uppermost love").[8]

Much of this framework had been formulated before him, but Thomas sharpened what he took over from his authors and provided it with definite shape and some new vocabulary. In particular, he held that love does not subsume the soul's knowledge of God into itself but actually discards it, in an act of transcendence which is unknowing (in a strong sense of the word): the unknowing of all creatures, of all knowledge, of all theology, of all categories; and the abandonment and forgetfulness even of the soul

---

[8] Not yet present in the *Exposicio* are two of the key terms in Gallus's fully-developed thought: *synderesis scintilla* (the spark of consciousness, or *Seelenfünklein*, as it was to become in later German mystical language: the spark of soul), and *apex mentis*, "the apex of the mind."

itself. He methodically interrelated two books of great authority: the MT, which would, he maintained, yield the entire theoretical part (*theorica*) of wisdom, and the Song of Songs, in which, he believed, Solomon had set out the practical (*practica*) side of the same.

A broad distinction can be drawn between two interpretations of the Pseudo-Dionysius which were to be found in the later Middle Ages.[9] The first of these is speculative in character and goes back to Albertus Magnus. The second, sometimes referred to as "affective Dionysianism," first attained its systematic formulation in the writings of Thomas Gallus. The value of the *Exposicio* in this regard should be appreciated, since in it the original kernel of Thomas's interpretation of the four books was unfolded: it was, in other words, the spring from which the broad current of his mystical thought was to flow in abundance.

Manuscripts

Five manuscripts are at present known to contain the glosses.[10]

① Vienna, *Staatsbibliothek 574*, fols 33–53

The folios which contain the glosses open with the misleading attribution, *Incipit prologus Johannis scoti in mysticam theologiam beati dionisii episcopi.* The prologue is in fact that of John Sarrazen. It is followed by the MT, which is divided up into short paragraphs each of which is followed (in the edition) by a gloss. The hand is of the fourteenth century.

② Besançon, *Bibliothèque municipale 167*, fols 45v–48r

The codex belonged to a Cistercian monastery. A commentary is copied for each of the four writings of the Pseudo-Dionysius, as well as two of the letters. On fol. 45vb the comment or gloss on the MT is announced: *Expositorium mistice theologie beati Dyonisii ariopagitici.* No attribution is made. It is a peculiarity of this MS that the glosses of Gallus on the four writings are presented divorced from the text of the MT.

---

[9] See Bernard McGinn, *The Flowering of Mysticism*, p. 79. See further Kurt Ruh, *Geschichte der abendländischen Mystik*, pp. 59–81.

[10] The possibility that more may turn up cannot be ruled out. For a fuller description and characterization of each manuscript consult my 2002 study of Eriugena and Gallus.

③ Zurich, *Zentralbibliothek C. 362*, fols 30r–34v

The manuscript, consisting of 34 folios of paper, was copied by Petrus Nümagen
(† 1505), whose hand is also exemplified in several other codices of the same library.
He performed this task sometime during the last quarter of the fifteenth century. He
did not attribute the glosses to any author. Despite its late date this MS presents a good
text. The glosses were identified in 1999 through a search conducted in connection
with the present edition.

④ Munich, *Staatsbibliothek Clm 7983*, fols 126v–130rb

This is a codex of the fourteenth century comprising 153 folios. The works of the
Pseudo-Dionysius begin on fol. 4r, while the glosses on the MT are found on fols
126v–130rb.
This MS gives its reader a truer sense of authenticity than any of the others. It was
made with great care. Its colorful decoration suggests Parisian origin. On each page the
text (in the version of Sarrazen) occupies the center while the glosses have been copied
around it in very orderly fashion by a separate hand. The MS belonged to the Cistercian monastery of Kaisheim in the diocese of Eichstätt (Germany), whence it came to
the royal library at Munich with the secularization of the years 1804–1806.

⑤ Dublin, *Milltown Park Jesuit Library, Phillipps 2800* (unfoliated)

This manuscript contains the four treatises of the Pseudo-Areopagite and the epistles in
the translation of Sarrazen, surrounded by the glosses. It is a direct copy in both layout
and text (in fact, in everything save decoration) of the Kaisheim text. It belonged to the
library of the Augustinian Canons at Rebdorf and was copied in the fourteenth century
by Fr. Jacob Siber. (Kaisheim and Rebdorf are only thirty kilometers apart as the crow
flies.) It was given to the Jesuit Library at Dublin in 1900. The identification of the
glosses as the work of Gallus was made in 2001 in connection with the present edition.

The Edition

All five manuscripts were employed in the preparation of this critical edition. The eval-
uation of their relative textual quality was arrived at on several grounds.
   In the first place the layout of the pages: M[unich] stood out in virtue of the care
with which each folio was formatted. The version of Sarrazen is written in the middle
of the page and the glosses are very evenly and tastefully distributed around it in a way
which suggests that it was intended faithfully to reproduce a model. In appearance,

therefore, it resembles many glossed Bibles. It is highly decorated, in a manner that suggests Parisian origin.[11] Besides that, it records the version and glosses on all four Pseudo-Dionysian works. Regarding MT, in particular, it contains all the elements which must have belonged to the autograph of Gallus: the prologue of John Sarrazen, the prologue of Gallus himself, the Sarrazen version, and the glosses by Gallus. D[ublin] equals it in all these ways because it is a direct copy of M. Z[urich] and V[ienna] lack the format of M — they simply copy version and gloss in alternation. B[esançon] has the prologue by Gallus, followed by the glosses but without the version. These considerations are external to the text, but they suggest as a preliminary hypothesis the superior fidelity of M.

Collation and comparison reveal that B differs considerably from MZ, and even from MZVD, the latter forming a group contrasting to B. This conclusion emerges from the following comparisons: [Prologus T.G.:] deus (B)/ipse deus (MZ); habitu B/habito respectu/MZ/; ad deum perveniendi (B)/perveniendi ad deum (MZ); [Gloss 2:] invcsti-gandi (B)/investigando (MZ); dici (B)/dicti MZ; deificare (B)/deificate (MZ); [Gloss 3:] corporalibus (B)/sensibilibus (MZ); existunt (B)/consistunt (MZ); [Gloss 4:] excedit (B)/excedunt (MZ); [Gloss 5:] speculatorum (B)/spectaculorum (MZ); successit in (B)/ascendit ad (MZ); [Gloss 6:] multas (B)/multarum (MZ); [Gloss 7:] sint (B)/sunt (MZ); viderint (B)/viderant (MZ); [Gloss 11:] ypothesibus (B)/ypotiposibus (MZVD); [Gloss 13:] mei (B)/nostri (MZ); loquendum (B)/eloquendum (MZ); dilatatur (B)/dilatabitur (MZ); descensui (B)/sensui (MZ); prolixitate (B)/prolixitatem (MZ); accessum (B)/excessum (MZ); [Gloss 15:] nec raciocinantur nec intelliguntur (B)/et raciocinantur et intelliguntur (MZ); [Gloss 16:] illi sit (B)/illi cause sit (MZ); creatorem et creaturam (B)/creaturam et creatorem (MZ); [Gloss 17:] nec ipsius (B)/nec est ipsius (MZ).

In two crucial cases MZ have the more difficult variant reading, which speaks for their general trustworthiness. 1. [Gloss 5:] *speculatorum* (B) is opposed to *spectaculorum* (in the other four) — a term which belongs to the key elements of Thomas Gallus's personal vocabulary. 2. [Gloss 11:] B has *ypothesibus*, whereas *ypotiposibus* (the other four) is the correct transcription of this unusual Greek word.

Manucript D may be left aside, for it was copied from M. So much is manifested by the fact that its variants add several misread words to all the variants already present in M. Examples of mistakes added are: [Gloss 2:] intelligencia (M)/intelligibilia (D); [Gloss 4:] substantivum (M)/subiectum (D, corr.); [Gloss 15:] substanciatum (M)/substantivatum (D).

---

[11] Note Grabmann's characterization of *MS Clm 7983*: "prachtvoll geschriebene, mit Initialen und Miniaturen ausgestattete Pergamenthandschrift aus der 2. Hälfte des XIII. Jhs." (Martin Grabmann, "Ein dem Petrus Hispanus zugeschriebener Kommentar," p. 1238).

Textually there is little to choose between M and Z. They differ rarely, but on one occasion Z has a better reading than M and B together: [Gloss 16:] nulli (Z)/nullo (BM).

V is really not a reliable manuscript, being the result of careless work. No reading of V alone has been retained in the edition.

From all these considerations M emerges as the most reliable manuscript, followed closely by Z, then by B and V (D, being a copy of M, gives no additional information). The edition follows the weighting thus accorded to the textual witnesses. Not all the variants occurring have been retained in the critical apparatus. Rather than assembling an exhaustive catalogue recording every error (for example, et/etiam, nec/neque) I have included variants which illustrate and manifest the relationships between and among the five witnesses to the text, and in doing so I have chosen to err upon the generous side.

On two occasions a word has been printed in our edition which does not occur in any of the manuscripts. Technically speaking these are two conjectures, but in fact they are not big risks. 1. [Gloss 7:] *unitur deo intellectualiter ignoto cognicione*: the manuscripts unanimously read *ignota*, by attraction with the feminine noun following the adjective, but in the parallel passage of the *Extractio* of Gallus *ignoto* is given; and it makes evidently better sense. 2. [Gloss 12:] *vestitum podere* [Apoc. 1:13]: the rare word *poderes* (or *poderis*), meaning a long robe descending to the ankle, defeated all our copyists, who have plumped for the easier *pondere* — not having taken the trouble to look up their Bible. In Gloss 2 the manuscript of MT which Gallus was following had the reading *dicti silentii* instead of the correct *docti silentii* (in the gloss he ingeniously referred "the silence of the divine Word" in order to make plausible sense of the contradiction). This edition naturally retains the word which Gallus read, even though it was not what Sarrazen wrote.

The chapter sub-sections are those which Gallus himself employed. Gallus prefaced each chapter with a useful thematic summary, beginning always with the authentic title which he took from the Sarrazen version. Scriptural references are printed in the edition of the gloss and are not repeated in the Latin text or the English translation. The orthography of M has been retained with only a few changes. Names have been given an initial capital. Gobbets of the version have been italicized (corresponding to underlinings in M and Z) in the glosses. Modern punctuation has been introduced and the glosses have been numbered 1 through 17. In Z different script sizes are used for the Dionysian text and the glosses, a convention that I have followed in the edition in order to insure that Gallus's work appears in the same format as Grosseteste's translation and commentary, which appears in the second half of this book.

I did not set out to make an edition of the *versio Sarraceni*, nor did I wish to reproduce the faulty Alonso text. Instead I have reprinted the text from Chevallier's

Dionysiaca.[12] However, I have bracketed [ ] in the text the readings which Gallus appears to have had in front of him, in those cases where the meaning of the gloss is directly affected. I have changed final *ae* of nouns and adjectives to *e*, in the medieval manner.

The text of the glosses has appeared in print in two editions. Floss printed them in P.L. 122 from the Vienna manuscript, with an attribution to Eriugena. Manuel Alonso, S.J., published them in 1957 under the name of Peter of Spain, using the Vienna and Munich manuscripts. (See Bibliography, p. 133.) My critical edition is based upon all five known witnesses to the text.

The English Translation of MT and of the Exposicio

Two very different English versions of MT have been consulted throughout the process of re-translating: Parker (1897) and Colm Luibheid (1987).[13] On the other hand the object of my translating exercise could not be satisfied by either style, since my aim was not to add to the existing translations from the Greek MT but to offer to the reader of the glossed Sarrazen version of MT a facing translation of the latter for purposes of reference. The English version printed here has therefore been based immediately upon the Latin of Sarrazen, though the Greek original has always been kept to hand for purposes of comparison. The choice of English vocabulary has been made with the Latin in mind, with the result that the translation has a Latin quality that is the result of a deliberate choice. Every translation is to some extent an interpretation. Where Luibheid brings out with skill the Plotinian and Proclean harmonics of the MT vocabulary (aspects of which the medieval student was naturally unconscious), Sarrazen employed when translating a vocabulary which paid a large tribute to the Vulgate and the Augustinian writings, and as a glossator Thomas Gallus overlaid upon the version his own distinctive mystical terminology, such as *apex mentis, affectio, industria* and *spectaculum*. These qualities I have sought to reproduce, in accordance with the very particular finality of our translation. For example, in different contexts, *substancia* is rendered as "being" or "substance"; the couplet *posicio et ablacio* is translated "positive attribution and removal," while *posicio* by itself is rendered as "assertion"; *ablacio* becomes "taking away," and *excessus* becomes "ecstasy" (except in expressions like *excessus luminis*). *Supersubstantialis* is translated by "beyond being," *excellentia* by "transcendence," and *remotio* by "removal."

---

[12] Reference in Bibliography.
[13] See Bibliography.

2. *De Mystica Theologia*: the Version of John Sarrazen (1166–1167) and the *Exposicio Vercellensis* (1233) — Latin Text

Manuscripts:

B Besançon, *Bibliothèque municipale 167*, fols 45v–48r (late 13th c.)
M Munich, *Staatsbibliothek Clm 7983*, fols 126v–130rb (2nd half of 13th c.)
Z Zurich, *Zentralbibliothek C.362*, fols 30r–34v (ca. 1500)
V Vienna, *Staatsbibliothek 574*, fols 33–53 (14th c.)
D Dublin, *Milltown Park Jesuit Library, Phillipps 2800* (ca. 1300; unfoliated)

[Prologus Ioannis Sarraceni]

Ante misticam theologiam "simbolica theologia" esset transferenda. Nam post librum "de divinis nominibus" ipsam esse conpositam ex verbis beati Dyonisii declaratur. Set in partibus illis Grecie, in quibus fui, ipsam solicite querens non inveni. Quod si forte per illum vestrum monachum qui in Greciam profectus esse dicitur ipsam et alios libros de quibus fratri Gulielmo verba feci obtinueritis rogo quatinus michi vestro clerico id designetis. Interim autem a me translatam, "misticam" suscipite "theologiam." Videtur autem dici mistica, quasi occulta et clausa, quia cum iuxta eam per ablaccionem ad Dei cognicionem ascenditur, tandem quid sit Deus clausum et occultum relinquitur. Potest eciam dici mistica, quia multa de Deo doctrina sic quoque conparatur. Myo, unde mistica dicitur, et claudo et disco et doceo interpretatur.

Prologus [Vercellensis]

Trinitas supersubstantialis, etc. Titulus huius libri est de mystica theologia.

3. English Translation

[Prologue of John Sarrazen]

The *Symbolic Theology* should have been translated before the *Mystical Theology*, for it is clear from the words of the Bl. Dionysius that it was composed after the book on the *Divine Names*. However, a diligent search made for it in the regions of Greece where I was, was unable to turn it up. If you should perchance obtain it through the agency of that monk of your community who is said to have journeyed to Greece, and along with it the other books about which I have spoken to Brother William, I am requesting you to let me know of it through your clerk. Meanwhile, receive my translation of the *Mystical Theology*. It appears to be termed "mystical" in the sense of "hidden" and "closed," on the grounds that when the ascent to the knowledge of God is made by its path through removal [of attributes], in the last analysis the nature of God is left closed and hidden. "Mystical" can also be used because much teaching about God is also approached thus. *Myo*, from which "mystic" comes, is translated by any of the following: "I close"; "I learn"; "I teach."

Prologue [of Thomas Gallus]

Trinitas supersubstancialis, etc. ["Trinity beyond being."] The title of this book is *On Mystical Theology*.

Dicitur autem mistica, id est clausa vel occulta, quia quicquid ibi dicitur quasi inexplicabile totum clausum et occultum relinquitur. Est autem huius libri materia ipse[1] Deus in se simpliciter consideratus, nullo habito respectu[2] reali ad creata. Intencio vero eius est commendare veram sapienciam christianorum et philosophorum sapienciam reprobare. Utilitas vero eius[3] est inducere ad apicem perfeccionis in via, id est uniri Deo per superintellectualem cognicionem et affeccionem, sive ut uno vocabulo dicatur utrumque per deificacionem. Forma vero sive modus tractandi talis est. Primo Deum invocat, ut per ipsum ad idipsum dirigatur. Secundo instruit Thimotheum quomodo vera sapiencia inquiratur, ibi: *tu autem, amice.* Tercio prohibet ne thesaurus istius sapiencie indignis ostendatur, innuens errorem quo impediuntur, ne vera ab eis sapiencia inveniatur, ibi: *Vide autem.* Quarto ostendit secundum diversas raciones et varias quod omnis creatura de Deo sine aliqua contrarietate affirmatur et negatur, ibi: *Oportet in ipsa.* Quinto demonstrat qui[4] sunt, quibus gratia perveniendi ad Deum per superintellectualem cognicionem donatur, ibi: *Etenim non simpliciter.*

Et haec omnia facit in primo capitulo.

Capitulum primum

[1] Titulus huius capituli est "Quod divina lux per divinam noctem aspicitur et ipsa divina nox per occasum luminum invenitur." Ibique quod est clarum obscuratur, quod est magnum coartatur, quod est humanum deificatur, et quod est ignotum magis ignoratur. *Divina lux* est divine cognicionis claritas; *divina nox* est ipsius cognicionis incomprehensibilitas, que cum *aspicitur* Deus cognoscitur. *Invenitur* autem ipsa incomprehensibilitas *per occasum luminum*, id est per excessum omnium sensuum et virium mentalium, quo obtento ipsa cognicio obscuratur, quia in excessum maioris cognicionis augmentatur, et latitudo verbi vocalis et mentalis restringitur in simplicitatem verbi eternalis. Ibi fit etiam deificacio, id est de humanis in divina transmutacio, et illud quod est ignotum per investigacionem racionis et intellectualis operacionis fit ignocius per excessum unicionis, ita tamen quod talis ignorancia summa est apud viatorem sciencia.

---

[1] ipse] *om.* B
[2] habito respectu] habitu B
[3] eius] *om.* BM
[4] qui] que B

Now it is called mystical, that is to say, closed or hidden, because whatever is said in it is left as it were without explanation, completely closed and hidden. The matter of this book is God himself considered simply in himself without regard of any kind to created things. Its aim, on the other hand, is to commend the true wisdom of Christians and to reject the wisdom of the philosophers. Its utility lies in bringing one to the high point of perfection on the pilgrimage [of this life], that is to say to be united to God through a knowledge and a love that are beyond intellect, or (to express both of these by one word) through deification. But the form or method of discussion is as follows. First he invokes God, so that through him he may be directed to him. Secondly, he instructs Timothy as to how the true wisdom may be pursued, where he says, *Tu autem, amice* ["But you, friend"]. Thirdly, he forbids opening the treasure-house of this wisdom to those unworthy of it, and hints at the error which impedes them from finding the true wisdom, where he says, *vide autem* ["But see"]. In the fourth place he uses various considerations and approaches to show that every creature may without any contradiction be affirmed and denied of God, where he says, *Oportet in ipsa* ["We are required to attribute to it"]. Fifthly, he shows who those people are to whom the grace of reaching God through superintellectual knowledge is granted, where he says, *Etenim non simpliciter* ["Yet it is not for nothing"].

All these points make up the first chapter.

Chapter I
[Title and summary]
[1] The title of this chapter is, "That the divine light is glimpsed through the divine night, and the divine night is discovered through the fading of the lights." When that happens, what is clear becomes obscure, what is great is reduced, what is human is deified, and what is unknown is even more unknown. The *divine light* is the clarity of the divine knowledge. The *divine night* is the incomprehensibility of that knowledge; God is known when this *is glimpsed*. The incomprehensibilty itself *is found through the fading of the lights*, that means by going beyond all the senses and the mental powers. Having got that far, knowledge itself is darkened since it is increased beyond itself towards greater knowledge. Also the breadth of the vocal word, or even of the mental one, is restricted to the simplicity of the eternal Word. And it is there also that deification occurs, that is to say, a changeover from human things to divine. Also, what is not known through the inquiry of the reason and the working of the intellect becomes still more unknown by the transcendence of becoming united; but in such a way that that very ignorance is the highest knowledge to which the wayfarer can attain.

[MT I.1: Versio Sarraceni]

Trinitas supersubstantialis et superdea et superbona, inspectrix divine sapientie Christianorum, dirige nos ad mysticorum eloquiorum superignotum, et supersplendentem et summum verticem, ubi simplicia et absoluta et inconvertibilia theologie mysteria cooperta sunt secundum supersplendentem occulte docti [dicti, T.G.] silentii caliginem, in obscurissimo superclarissimum supersplendere facientem, et in omnino impalpabili et invisibili superpulchris claritatibus superimplentem non habentes oculos mentes. Igitur ista mihi quidem sint oratione postulata.

[2] *Trinitas supersubstancialis* etc., usque ad illud *tu autem* etc. talis est sensus.

O trina unitas et una trinitas divinarum videlicet personarum, superexcedens omne ens quo ad personam Patris, et superexcedens omnem scienciam et sapienciam quo ad personam Filii, et superexcedens omnem existentem bonitatem quo ad personam Spiritus Sancti; que inspiciendo approbas et approbando inspicis sapienciam fidelium qua Deus cognoscitur, que scilicet est optima portio Mariae [cf. Lk 10:42]. Directo radio a te ad nos, nos ad te elevando rege ut perveniamus ad te per contemplacionem qui es summus vertex sacrarum scripturarum, nobis quidem *superignotus* in te autem supersplendens, in quo, videlicet summe altissimo *vertice*, sentencie sacre scripture profundissime sunt clause et abscondite et sicut in arte simplicissima coartate, et a verborum velaminibus absolute. Unde quoniam sunt *simplices* sunt et *inconvertibiles*, id est tantum uno modo intelligibiles. Sunt autem in isto vertice *cooperte* iste sentencie secundum lucem que habet excessum luminis [cf. I Tim 6:16], et ideo sortitur nomen *caliginis*, cuius splendor occultus est, verbum eternum quod Pater inaudibiliter ab aeterno loquitur [cf. Iob 33:14]. Quod quidem in illa summa invisibilitate Deum, qui est *superclarissimus*, facit desuper radiantem, et in illo statu ubi nec racio investigando[5] palpat nec intelligencia[6] contemplando considerat, radiis eternaliter simplicibus et effectualiter multiplicibus superfundit celestes mentes, que sibi tote sunt oculus, vel quae non utuntur materialibus sensibus. Et ista sunt que per modum oracionis a Deo postulo; quoniam non aliter intelliguntur nisi per oracionem, a Deo impetrentur.

---

[5] investigando] investigandi B
[6] intelligencia] intelligibilia D

[MT I.1]

Trinity beyond being, beyond divinity and goodness, guardian of Christians' divine wisdom! Show us the way towards that highest peak of mystical Scriptures exalted above unknowing and beyond brightness! There the simple, absolute and changeless mysteries of the Word of God are covered in the brilliant darkness of a secretly-spoken silence, making the transcendent clarity shine (and more than shine!) in the darkest place, and in the wholly unsensed and unseen, completely filling sightless minds with brightness beyond all beauty. These things, therefore, are indeed requested by me in prayer.

[Gloss]
[2] *Trinitas supersubstancialis*, etc. ["Trinity beyond being"], down to *Tu autem*, etc. ["but you"]: this is the meaning.

O threefold unity and unique Trinity of the divine persons, exceeding by far every being as far as the person of the Father is concerned, and, equally far, all knowledge and wisdom with regard to the person of the Son, and, equally, every existing goodness with regard to the person of the Holy Spirit: by your guardianship you approve the wisdom of the faithful through which God is known, and by approving you guard it. This in fact is the best portion of Mary. Rule us by the ray directed from you to us, lifting us up to you so that we may reach you through contemplation. You are the highest peak of the sacred Scriptures, to us *more than unknown* but in yourself beyond brightness. And on that highest of high *peaks* the authoritative utterances of sacred Scripture are closed, hidden in the deep depths, compressed as though in the most simple art, and cut off from the veils of words. Whence, since they are *simple* they are also *unchanging*, that is, there is only one way of understanding them. However, those authoritative utterances are *covered over* upon that peak, with regard to the light which has an excess of light — and therefore it is given the name of *darkness*. Its hidden splendor is the eternal Word which the Father inaudibly speaks from eternity. In that exalted invisibility, [the Word] makes God, who is above clarity, radiate downwards, and in that state which neither the reason touches by inquiry nor intelligence considers in contemplation, those rays which are eternally simple yet multiple in their effects [the Word] pours over the celestial minds, which to themselves are all eye (or do not use material senses). And these are the things which I ask of God through prayer, for these are things that are not understood in any other way than by being requested of God in prayer.

Nota quod vertex secretorum divinorum dicitur *superignotus, supersplendens* et *summus*. *Superignotus* dicitur, quia ad ipsum racio deficit per investigacionem; *supersplendens* dicitur, quia ad ipsum intellectus deficit per superfluentem luminis effusionem; *summus* vero dicitur, quia ad ipsum intelligencia deficit per excedentem affeccionis unicionem. Ibi sentencie sacre scripture sunt *simplices*, quia sicut videntur intelliguntur; sunt *absolute*, quia nullis elementorum velaminibus detinentur; sunt *inconvertibiles*, quia ad hunc vel illum intellectum non reducuntur; sunt *cooperte*, quia superlucenti lumine obteguntur. Quod lumen dicitur a beato Dyonisio *supersplendens occulte dicti silentii caligo*. Haec est divina incomprehensibilitas, que dicitur *caligo* propter luminis excessionem; dicitur *occulte supersplendens* propter intimam, vel in intimis sanctam luminis supereffusionem; *dicti*[7] etiam dicitur propter verbum eternum quod Pater ab eterno loquitur. Dicitur *silencii* propter quod generacio talis verbi ab intellectuali auditu non percipitur, unde quia auditui mentis non est perceptibilis, ideo a verbo oris non est enarrabilis. Ysaias: *generationem eius quis enarrabit?* [Is 53:8; cf. Act 8:33], quasi diceret, nullus. Et in illo statu obscurissimo per excessum luminis Deus, qui est clarissimus[8] per naturam, fit menti supersplendens per radiorum habundanciam. Ibi racio nihil *palpat*, quia nihil est ibi investigabile; ibi intellectus[9] nihil *videt*, quia nihil est ibi contemplabile, et tamen *superpulchris lucibus* divine refulgencie superimplentur, se ipsas per se ipsas et alia a seipsis videntes, humane et angelice deificate[10] intelligencie.

[MT I.2]

Tu autem, o amice Timothee, circa mysticas visiones forti contritione et sensus derelinque, et intellectuales operationes, et omnia sensibilia et intelligibilia, et omnia non exsistentia et exsistentia; et sicut est possibile, ignote consurge ad eius unitionem qui est super omnem substantiam et cognitionem. Etenim excessu tui ipsius et omnium irretentibili et absoluto munde, ad supersubstantialem divinarum tenebrarum radium, cuncta auferens et a cunctis absolutus sursum ageris.

---

[7] dicti] dici B
[8] clarissimuss] carissimus M
[9] intellectus] nullus D
[10] deificate] deificari B

Note that the peak of the divine secrets is said to be *beyond knowledge, beyond brightness and beyond height*. It is called *beyond knowledge*, because reason in its inquiry fails at it; it is called *beyond brightness*, because the intellect fails at it in virtue of the downflow and outpouring of light; it is said to be *beyond height*, because the intelligence fails at it in virtue of the transcendent uniting of affection. There the authoritative utterances of the sacred Scripture are *simple*, because they are understood as they seem to be; they are *absolute*, because they are not held down by any veils of the elements; they are *unchanging*, because they are not reduced to this or that understanding; they are *covered over*, because they are protected by the brilliantly-shining light. This light is referred to by the Bl. Dionysius as the *intensely-shining darkness of the hiddenly spoken silence*. This is the divine incomprehensibility, which is called darkness because of the transcendence of the light. It is called *shining (and more than shining)* in the dark, because of the intimate (or inward) holy downpouring of the light. It is also called *spoken*, because of the eternal Word which the Father speaks from eternity. It is called *silence,* since the generation of this Word is not perceived by intellectual audition. Since it is not perceptible to the hearing of the mind, it is therefore not able to be spoken by the word of the mouth either. Isaiah: *Who shall tell his generation?* — as though to say, no one! In that state, which is very dark by the transcendence of light, God, who is the most clear light by nature, comes to be shining down upon the mind through the abundance of rays. There reason *touches* nothing, because nothing is subject to inquiry there. There the intellect *sees* nothing, because nothing is able to be contemplated there. And nevertheless the human and angelic deified intelligences are filled (and more than filled) *by the very beautiful lights* of the divine shining, and through themselves they see themselves and other things than themselves.

[MT I.2]

But you, Timothy my friend, by a mighty struggle regarding the mystical visions, leave behind the operations of sense and intellect and all objects of sense and understanding, all that is and all that is not; and, without knowledge, strive upward as much as you can towards becoming united with the One who is above all being and knowledge. For, removing all things and being freed from them all, by an irresistible and absolute ecstasy relative to yourself and all things you will be uplifted to the ray of the divine shadows which is above all being.

[3] *Tu autem amice* usque ad illud *vide autem*, talis est sensus.

Tu, Thimothee, qui per verum amorem alter ego michi factus es, ut possis intelligere secretas contemplaciones de quibus te modo cupio instruere, sic cooperare radio divino ut forti mentis conamine derelinquas usus *sensuum* corporalium cum sensibilibus[11] exerciciis, *et intellectuales operaciones* et animas et angelicas substancias, *et omnia* que de verbo eterno in esse prodierunt, et omnia que in solo verbo superessenciali consistunt,[12] que scilicet in ipso verbo sunt contemplabilia; et sunt omnia transeunda. Et sicut tua requirit possibilitas, scienter nescius quo non videt oculus, *consurge* per principalem affeccionem *ad* dei *unicionem*,[13] *qui est super omnem substanciam* ineffabiliter collocatus, et super omnem *cognicionem* tam humanam quam angelicam incomprehensibiliter collocatus. *Etenim* cum *te ipsum* et[14] omnia alia mente *excesseris* ita quod illorum amore retineri non valeas, vel alias impediri, purgatus ab ultimis anime fantasiis tam spiritales quam divinas operaciones postponendo, elevaberis ad superclarissimum lumen occultissime deitatis, quae videlicet dicitur *tenebra* [cf. Ps 18:11] quia sic videtur quod non videtur, vel quia sic intelligitur a nobis quod non comprehenditur.

[MT I.3]

Vide autem ut nullus indoctorum ista audiat; istos autem dico, qui in exsistentibus sunt formati, nihil super exsistencia supersubstantialiter esse opinantes, sed putantes scire ea que secundum ipsos est cognitione eum qui ponit tenebras latibulum suum [Ps 17: 12]. Si autem super istos sunt divine doctrine mysteriorum, quid dicat quidem aliquis de magis indoctis, quicumque omnibus superpositam causam et ex postremis in exsistentibus figurant et nihil ipsam habere dicunt super compositas ab ipsis impias et multiformes formationes?

---

[11] sensibilibus] corporalibus B
[12] consistunt] existunt B
[13] unicionem] *corr. in* imitacionem D
[14] et] ad B

[Gloss]

[3] *Tu autem, amice*, etc. ["But you, friend"], up to *vide autem*, etc. ["But see"]: this is the meaning.

You, Timothy, who through true love have become an *alter ego* to me: to be able to understand the secret contemplations about which I want now to instruct you, cooperate with the divine ray so that by a mighty struggle of the mind you may leave behind the use of the corporeal senses together with the activities of the senses, *and the intellectual operations*, and souls and angelic beings, *and all things* that have come into being from the eternal Word, and also all things which exist together in the one and only Word-beyond-being: those things namely which can be contemplated in the Word itself, and which are all to be transcended. And rise up just as may be possible for you, in knowing ignorance, to where the eye cannot reach; *rise* by means of the principal affection *towards being united* with God *who is* located incomprehensibly beyond speech *above all being*, and is located incomprehensibly above all *knowing*, either human or angelic. *For indeed*, when in the mind you *go beyond yourself* and all other things, so that you cannot any longer be held back by the love of them or impeded by any other thing, purified from the lowest images of the soul by putting behind you both the spiritual and the divine operations, you will be raised up to the light of the deeply-hidden deity — light that is beyond all brightness. This, of course, is called *shadow*, because in this way is seen what is not seen, or because in this way is understood by us what is not comprehended.

[MT I.3]

But see that none of the uninformed should hear those things: I mean those people who are formed in beings, supposing that there is nothing transcendently beyond the beings, but thinking that they know with the knowledge that is theirs the One "who has made the shadows his hiding place." But if the divine teachings of the mysteries are beyond them, what indeed is one to say about the even more uninformed, those who portray the cause located above all things in terms of the lowest of existing things and who also say that it has nothing over and beyond the impious and multiformed shapes composed by themselves?

[4] *Vide autem ubi nullus* usque *oportet in ipsa*, talis est sensus.

Cave, ne aliquis incredulorum aut inexpertorum ista secreta audiat. *Istos autem dico* qui naturalibus racionibus aut amori[15] *existencium* firmiter innituntur, existimantes quod *nihil* sit *super* ens, quod dicitur subiectum metaphysice[16] tam creata quam increata continens, iuxta suam opinionem. Et hoc habent[17] ex illo verbo quod dicitur in Exodo, *Ego sum qui sum* [Ex 3:14]. Sed hoc dictum est ut in primo intellectu se offeret nobis, quasi quoddam memoriale, ut se computaret nobiscum habere esse, qui erat totaliter super esse. Et hii tales putant per investigacionem creaturarum, que eis connaturalis est, pervenire ad eius cognicionem vel divinam comprehensionem, qui per supersubstancialitatem suam omni cognitioni se subtrahit et comprehensioni. Si autem doctrine divinorum occultorum scientiam tantorum philosophorum excedunt,[18] quam magis excedet impericiam illorum qui Deum, qui est superposita omnium causa, ex extremis materiis existencium figurant, que inferiora sunt animatis. Nec insuper putant quod Deus in se aliquid habeat sublimius quam figure et forme multiplices que ab ipsis impie componuntur.

[MT I.4]

Oportet enim in ipsa et omnes exsistentium ponere et affirmare positiones sicut omnium causa, et omnes ipsas magis proprie negare super omnia superexsistente, et non negationes oppositas opinari esse affirmationibus, sed multo prius ipsam super privationes esse, que est super omnem et ablationem et positionem. Ita igitur divinus Bartholomeus dicit et multam theologiam esse et minimam, et evangelium latum et magnum, et rursus concisum. Mihi videtur illud supernaturaliter intendens quia et multorum sermonum est bona omnium causa et brevium dictionum simul et irrationabilis: sicut neque rationem habens neque intellectum, propter hoc quod omnibus ipsa supersubstantialiter est superposita, et solis non velate

---

15 amori] amore B
16 subiectum metaphysice] substantivum V substantia Z
17 habent] dicunt B
18 excedunt] excedit B

[Gloss]

[4] *Vide autem ubi nullus*, etc. ["But see that none"] up to *oportet in ipsa*, etc. ["We are required"]: this is the meaning.

Take care lest one of the unbelieving or the inexperienced should hear those secrets. *I mean people* who firmly depend upon natural reasons or the love *of existent things*, thinking that there is *nothing above* being — understood as the subject of metaphysics and containing both created and uncreated realities, according to their opinion. And this they have from the word that is spoken in Exodus, *I am who am*. But this was spoken so that he might offer himself in a first understanding to us as a kind of reminder, that he might count himself to have being along with us, he who was completely above being. And people of this kind think that through the investigation of creatures, which is connatural to them, they can arrive at the knowledge or divine comprehension of the One who withdraws himself from all knowledge and comprehension, by virtue of being beyond being. If, however, the doctrines of the divine hidden things transcend the knowledge of such great philosophers, how much more will they transcend the unlearnedness of those who portray God (who is the cause placed beyond all things) by reliance upon the lowest material beings, which are beneath the level of life! Moreover, they do not think that God has in himself something more sublime than the figures and multiple forms which they impiously compose.

[MT I.4]

We are required to attribute to it all the positive attributes of existent things and to affirm them of it, since it is the cause of all; and more appropriately still to deny all of these, since it exists far beyond all things. We are not to suppose that the negations are opposed to the affirmations. Instead we should hold that, being above every removal and every positive attribution, it is prior by far to the privative [use of] terms. And therefore the Bl. Bartholomew says that the word of God is both vast and tiny, and the Gospel broad and great, and yet concise. He seems to me to have comprehended this supernaturally: that the good cause of things is both of many words and brief ones, and at the same time irrational — meaning by that having neither reason nor intellect. On this account it is placed high above all things as being beyond being, and it appears unveiled and truly only to those who go beyond things both impure and pure, and who mount above every ascent of all holy summits, and who leave behind all

et vere apparet his qui et immunda et munda transeunt et omnem omnium sanctarum extremitatum ascensum superveniunt, et omnia divina lumina et sonos et sermones celestes derelinquunt, et ad caliginem introeunt, ubi vere est, sicut eloquia dicunt, qui est super omnia [Ex 20:21; cf. Ex 19].

[5] *Oportet in ipsa* usque *Etenim*, talis est sensus.

Quamvis illi ita senserint, tamen necesse est secundum rectam intelligenciam omnem formam vel figuram vel substanciam, et omnem omnino creaturam non tanquam subiecto, sed sicut *omnium causae* ipsi attribuere, et magis proprie et veraciter ab ea removere, sicut rei cui nihil existencium inherere potest secundum quod Deus. Et quamvis existencia Deo attribuantur vel ab eo removeantur, non tamen credendum est quod inter talem affirmacionem vel negacionem cadat aliqua contrarietas, immo eciam oportet sentire ipsam omnium causam superiorem esse omni negacioni aut affirmacioni. Unde de ea non potest esse aliqua posicio vel ablacio, sive affirmatio vel negatio. Et iuxta hanc consideracionem beatus *Bartholomeus* Deo conformis scribit theologiam esse prolixam in verbis et coartatam in sensibus, et evangelium *latum* in parabolis *et magnum* in historiis, et rursus artum et parvum in mysteriis. Per hoc autem dico beatum Bartholomeum divina sapiencia plenum supermundanum intellectum habuisse, videlicet quod ipse Deus, qui *est bona omnium causa, multis sermonibus* designatur, et iterum paucissimis, in eo quod nec racione capitur nec intellectu comprehenditur, et ideo verbis non exprimitur. Ubi enim deficit verbum mentis deest et verbum oris. Ideo autem nec[19] mente capitur nec ore exprimitur quia *omnibus supersubstancialiter superponitur*. Illis autem solis sine velamine *apparet*, scilicet per infusam dulcedinem et suavitatem inpermixtam, qui omnia sensibilia et intelligibilia per excessum mentis transcendunt, et superant omnem[20] *ascensum* divinorum et intelligibilium obiectorum sive spectaculorum,[21] in quibus scilicet intellectualis contemplacionis exercicium consumatur, et omnes irradiaciones ad intellectum pertinentes et inspiraciones ambiguas et revelaciones certas *derelinquunt*, et intrant per unicionem ad superintellectualem dei incomprehensibilitatem, ubi in propria forma secundum testimonia scripture est deus, qui est super unum et unitatem et super ens et entitatem. Dicitur enim in Exodo quod Moyses *ascendit ad*[22] *caliginem, in qua erat Deus* [Ex 20:21].

---

[19] nec] non B
[20] omnem] omnes B
[21] spectaculorum MZVD] speculatorum B
[22] ascendit ad] accessit in B

divine lights and sounds and heavenly words and enter into the darkness where, as the Scripture says, he truly is who is above all.

[Gloss]
[5] *Oportet in ipsa* ["We are required"] down to *Etenim* ["Yet"]: this is the meaning.

Although that is the way they think, nevertheless according to a proper understanding it is necessary to attribute to it the form of all things or their shape or their substance, and every creature universally — not as though to a subject but to the cause of all things; and more properly and truly to remove [them] from it, as from a reality in which, in so far as it is God, no particular existent can inhere. And even though existent things may be attributed to God or be removed from him, it is not to be believed that some [logical] opposition should hold between an affirmation and a negation of this kind. Instead we should also maintain that the cause of all things is above every negation and affirmation. Hence there cannot be any positive attribution to it or any removal (or affirmation or negation). Going by this consideration Bl. *Bartholomew*, the one close to God, writes that theology is prolix in words and narrowed in meanings, and that the Gospel is *broad* in parables and *great* in histories and, on the other hand, narrow and small in mysteries. For this reason, however, I say that Bl. Bartholomew had an understanding, beyond this world and full of divine wisdom, to the effect that God himself, who *is the good cause of all things*, is designated by *many words*, and again by very few; due to the fact that he is neither captured by reason nor comprehended by intellect, and thus is not expressed in words. For where the word of the mind is failing the word of the mouth is likewise. But on that account he is neither captured by the mind nor expressed by the mouth, because *he is beyond all things* through being beyond being. To those alone does he *appear* without a veil, that is to say, by an infused softness and unmixed sweetness, who transcend all sensibles and intelligibles through ecstasy of the mind, and who mount above every *ascent* of divine and intelligible objects or showings; [those in whom] the exercise of intellectual contemplation is consummate, and who *leave* all the enlightenments pertaining to the intellect, and ambiguous inspirations and certain revelations; and enter, through uniting, into the incomprehensibility of God which is beyond understanding. There in his own form, according to the testimonies of Scripture, is the God who is above one and unity, and being and entity. For it is said in Exodus that Moses *went up into the darkness in which God was*.

[MT I.5]

Etenim non simpliciter divinus Moyses mundari ipse primum precipitur, et rursus a non talibus segregari, et post omnem mundationem audit multarum vocum buccinas, et videt lumina multa cum fulgore emittentia mundos et multum effusos radios [cf. Ex 19; 20: 18–21]. Postea a multis segregatur, et cum electis sacerdotibus ad summitatem divinarum ascensionum pertingit. Quamvis per haec quidem non fit cum Deo, sed contemplatur non ipsum, invisibilis est enim, sed locum ubi est.

[6] *Etenim non simpliciter* usque *hec autem*, talis est sensus.

Ista quae supra diximus de transcensu divinorum luminum et sonorum et sermonum et introitu in caliginem, in ipso *Moyse* tipice sunt ostensa, qui non solum in seipso *mundari* iubetur ut Deum pre ceteris alcius contempletur, sed etiam ab immundis vel sibi dissimilibus separari. *Et post omnem* purgacionem sensuum a sensibilibus et intellectus a fantasmatibus, *audit* sive mente percipit multarum[23] intelligenciarum inspiraciones, et contemplatur multa spectacula luculentissima, desuper habundanti plenitudine emanancia cum candore radios, in substancia simplices et in intelligencia multiplices. Tandem *segregatus* a multitudine populari, id est multipharia opinione materiali, cum principalibus affectionibus ascendit ad Deum [Ex 19:3] videndum. Cuius tamen substanciam non vidit,[24] cum sit invisibilis, *sed locum ubi est* Deus, sive ipse locus sit celum serenum sive opus lapidis saphiri sive ignis ardens sive cacumen montis.

[MT I.6]

Hoc autem puto significare divinissima visorum et intellectorum esse subiectas quasdam rationes subiectorum omnia excedenti, per que presentia eius qui est super omnem cogitationem monstratur intelligibilibus

---

[23] multarum] multas B
[24] vidit] videt B

[MT I.5]

Yet it is not for nothing that the Bl. Moses is commanded first to be purified himself and then to be separated from those who are not pure. And
after the whole purification he hears the many-voiced trumpets; he sees the
many lights with the flash, emitting pure and abundantly-streaming rays.
Afterwards he is segregated from the crowd and reaches the summit of the
divine ascents with the chosen priests, even though he is not by that fact
with God, but he contemplates not him — for he is invisible — but the
place where he is.

[Gloss]
[6] *Etenim non simpliciter*, etc. ["Yet it is not for nothing"] down to *Hec autem*, etc. ["I
take it, however"]: this is the meaning.

What was said above about transcending the divine lights and sounds and words,
and about the entry into the darkness, is shown in *Moses* himself as in a type. He is commanded not only *to be cleansed* in himself, that he may contemplate God more highly
above the others, but also to be separated from the impure or those unlike to himself.
And following the whole purgation of the senses from sensibles and of the intellect from
phantasms *he hears*, or perceives in the mind, the inspiration of many intelligences, and
he contemplates many of the most splendid showings, sending out with radiance from
that superabundant fullness rays that are simple in substance and multiple in intelligence.
At last, *separated* from the multitude of the people, that is, from the multifarious operation of the material [power], with the principal affections he ascends to see God. But
he did not see his substance, since he is invisible, but *the place where* God *is*; whether
the place itself is the serene heaven, or the work of the sapphire stone, or the burning
fire or the mountain peak.

[MT I.6]

I take it, however, that this signifies that the most divine of the things seen
and contemplated are some lower-lying ideas of things subject to the One
who transcends all. Through them his presence, which is above all knowledge, is shown reaching to the highest intelligible summits of his most
holy places. And then [Moses] is set free from what is seen and sees, and
enters into the darkness of ignorance. This darkness truly is mystical. In

summitatibus sanctissimorum locorum eius superveniens. Tunc et ab ipsis absolvitur visis et videntibus, et ad caliginem ignorantie intrat, que caligo vere est mystica, in qua claudit omnes cognitivas susceptiones, et in non palpabili omnino et invisibili fit, omnis exsistens eius qui est super omnia, et nullius, neque sui ipsius, neque alterius, omnino autem ignoto, vacatione omnis cognitionis, secundum melius unitus, et eo quod nihil cognoscit super mentem cognoscens.

[7] *Hoc autem puto* usque in finem capituli, talis est sensus.

Dictum est Deum non videri sed locum ubi est, id est in creaturis quibusdam que dicuntur esse divinissima subiecta visorum et intellectorum vel divinissima loca, quia nihil divinius mente intuemur. Quibus arbitror designari summas et eternas architipias sive raciones aut exemplaria omnium creaturarum Deo subiectarum, per quas Deus fit presens et cognitive nobis manifestatur, se ipsum nobis desuper infundens et manifestans principaliores et superiores intelligencias earumdem racionum, que utcunque sunt[25] a nobis per speculum intelligibiles. Postea *Moyses separatur* ab hiis qui secum locum Dei viderant,[26] id est ab omnibus intelligibilibus operacionibus, et subtrahitur ab omni intelligencia activa et passiva,[27] sive ab omni obiecto intellectuali et visu mentali, et intrat *ad caliginem ignorancie*, quia unitur incomprehensibilitati divine quam apex intelligentie non penetrat, *que caligo vere est mystica*, id est clausiva, quia vere est omnis cognicionis clausiva et in se *claudit* et secretissime celat omnes comprehensivas cogniciones sicut in prima omnium causa. Et per hanc caliginem omnis animus unitus Deo *qui est super omnia*, fit in statu excellentissimo quem nec[28] ratio palpat per investigacionem nec intellectus contemplatur per visionem, per quem etiam statum ab omnibus aliis et a se ipso separatur quantum ad intellectualem proprie cognicionis presenciam, et per unicionem dileccionis quae est effectiva universe cognicionis, unitur Deo intellectualiter ignoto[29] cognicione que multo melior est quam sit cognicio intellectualis. Et in eo quod intellectualem cognicionem dereliquit, *super* intellectum et *mentem* Dominum *cognoscit*, id est per sapienciam intellectualem quae superat donum intellectus [cf. Is 11:2]. Illa enim Deum cognoscit per unicionem, hec vero per raciones verbi.

---

[25] sunt] sint B
[26] viderant] viderint B
[27] passiva] passivo B
[28] nec] non B
[29] ignoto] ignota MSS

this state he closes off all that the mind may receive, and enters into the altogether intangible and invisible, belonging completely to him who is beyond everything, and belonging to no [other], neither himself nor anyone else. And through complete liberation from all knowledge, united in his better part to the altogether Unknown, he is knowing beyond the mind — by knowing nothing.

[Gloss]
[7] *Hec autem puto*, etc. ["I take it, however"], down to the end of the chapter: this is the meaning.

It was said that God is not seen but only the place where he is, that is, in certain creatures which are said to be the most divine subjects of what is seen and understood, or the most divine places, because we see nothing more divine with our mind. By these I think those highest and eternal archetypes are designated which are ideas or exemplars of all creatures subject to God. Through these [ideas] God becomes present and is manifested to us cognitively, pouring himself down upon us and manifesting the more primordial and higher intelligences of those very ideas, which in some way or other are intelligible to us through a mirror. Afterwards *Moses is separated* from those who along with him had seen the place of God, that is, from all intellectual operations, and is withdrawn from all intelligence active and passive, and from every intellectual object and mental sight; and he enters *into the darkness of ignorance* because he is united to the divine incomprehensibility, which the apex of our intelligence does not penetrate. *This darkness truly is mystical*, that is, closing over; because truly it *closes over* all knowledge, and closes in itself and most secretly hides all comprehending knowledge, as in the first cause of all things. And through this darkness every mind united to God *who is above all things* comes into the highest and best state, which neither the reason touches through investigation nor the intellect contemplates through vision. Also through this state he is separated from all others, and from himself as regards the intellectual presence of his own knowledge. And through the uniting of love which brings about all knowledge he is united to God, who is not known intellectually, by a knowledge which is much better than intellectual knowledge. And by leaving behind intellectual knowledge *he knows* God *beyond* intellect and *mind*, that is, by an intellectual wisdom which is superior to the gift of the intellect: the former knows God through uniting, but the latter through the ideas of the Word.

Capitulum secundum

[8] Titulus huius capituli est "Quomodo oportet uniri et ymnos referre omnium cause." Status unicionis non potest aliter optineri nisi per ferventissimum desiderium mentalis oracionis, et per virtutem supermentalis affeccionis ad quam non attingit oculus intellectualis cognicionis; unde talis cognicio dicitur fieri per ignoranciam. Proprius autem ymnus sive modus Deum laudandi est per negacionem sive remocionem, sicut est videre in figura lignea a qua quanto magis exterior grossicies removetur tanto magis pulcritudo figure videtur. Modus vero huius laudis est incipere ab inferioribus usque ad superiora ascendendo.

[MT II.1]

In hac superlucenti caligine fieri nos precamur, et per non videre et per ignorare videre et cognoscere eum qui est super omnem visionem et cognitionem, in ipso non videre et non cognoscere, et supersubstantialem supersubstantialiter laudare per omnium exsistentium ablationem; sicut ipsius nature insigne facientes, auferentes prohibitiones officientes munde occulti visioni; et ipsam in se ipsa ablatione sola occultam manifestantes pulchritudinem.

[9] *In hac superlucenti* etc. usque ad illud *Oportet* etc., talis est sensus.

Toto mentis affectu exoptamus[30] nos fieri *in caligine superlucenti*, id est in statu superintellectuali, qui lucidior est quam intellectualis, ut per mentis excessum in quo intellectus *non videt* nec aliquo modo *cognoscit*, possimus Deum *cognoscere et videre* superintellectualiter, per remocionem videlicet intellectualis cognicionis, cum ipse Deus visu intellectuali nullatenus attingatur. Et precamur nos *laudare* posse *supersubstancialem supersubstancialiter*, id est Deum, qui excedit omnem substanciam et omne[31] ens, *per ablacionem omnium existencium*; sicut est videre in artificibus qui aliquam fabricant similitudinem de qualibet inanimata materia, qui sculpendo et incidendo removent

---

[30] exoptamus] exoptacio B
[31] omne] esse B

Chapter II
[Title and summary]
[8] The title of this chapter is, "How it is necessary to be united to the cause of all and to give back praise." The state of uniting cannot be obtained otherwise than through the most fervent desire of mental prayer and through the power of an affection beyond the mind, one to which the eye of intellectual knowledge does not attain. For this reason such knowledge is said to come about through ignorance. But the proper praise or method of praising God is through negation or removal, as can be seen in [the case of] the wooden statue: the more the exterior roughness is removed from it the more the beauty of the shape is seen. The method of this praise, on the other hand, is to begin from the lower things, ascending to the higher ones.

[MT II.1]

We pray to come to this darkness beyond brightness, and by not seeing and not knowing to see and know the One who is beyond vision and knowledge in the not seeing and the not knowing; and to praise the One who is beyond being in a way that is beyond being through the taking away of all existing things — just as those who make a statue from life take away the encumbrances to the pure sight of what is hidden, and in the very act of taking away they bring to light the hidden beauty.

[Gloss]
[9] *In hac superlucenti*, etc. ["In this darkness beyond brightness"] down to *Oportet*, etc. ["We should"]: this is the meaning.

   We desire with the whole affection of the mind to be *in the darkness beyond brightness*, that is, in that state above intellect which is brighter than the intellectual [state], so that through an ecstasy of the mind in which the intellect *does not see* nor in any way *know*, we may be able *to know* God *and to see* him in a way beyond intellect; that is to say through the removal of intellectual knowledge, since God himself is in no way attained by intellectual sight. And we pray that we may be able *to praise* the One *who is beyond being in a way that is beyond being*, that is, God who is beyond every substance and every being, *through the taking away of all existent things*; as we see in artists, who make a likeness out of some inanimate matter: by sculpting and cutting they remove the outer, rougher parts of the material which hide and cover over, so that that pure image cannot be seen which naturally and potentially is within. And by the simple

exteriores partes materie grossiores, que occultant et cooperiunt ne videri possit illa pura ymago quae naturaliter et potencialiter est interius; et per solam talium offendiculorum remocionem sine alio additamento manifestatur in propria specie ipsius ymaginis *pulchritudo*, que prius latebat in *occulto*.

[MT II.2]

Oportet autem, sicut arbitror, ablationes laudare contrarie quam positiones; etenim illas, et a primis incipientes et per media ad ultima descendentes, ponebamus; hic autem, ab ultimis ad principaliora ascensus facientes, et per media rursus ad extrema, omnia auferimus ut revelate cognoscamus illam ignorantiam, ab omnibus noscibilibus in omnibus exsistentibus circumvelatam, et supersubstantialem illam videamus caliginem, ab omni lumine in exsistentibus occultatam.

[10] *Oportet autem sicut* usque in finem capituli, talis est sensus.

In premissis libris Deum laudavi per affirmaciones, in isto autem oportet laudare per negaciones et omnium ablaciones quasi contrario modo. Ibi enim inchoantes ab affirmacione vel posicione principaliorum *per media ad ultima* descensum faciebamus. *Hic autem ab ultimorum* ablacione incipientes usque ad ablacionem *principaliorum* gradatim per media ascendimus, et iterum ad postrema reflexi omnia ab eo pariter *auferemus*, quod ideo facimus ut sine velo mystice significacionis *cognoscamus* divinam incomprehensibilitatem latentem sub misticis velis *omnium existencium* que possunt a nobis cognosci vel cogitari. Insuper hoc facimus ut contemplemur divinam incomprehensibilitatem que excedit omne ens: que videlicet *occultata est* ab omni[32] sciencia in omnibus creaturis.

---

[32] occultata est ab omni] collocata est ab omnibus B

removal of such encumbrances, without any adding on, the beauty of the image itself is manifested in its own visible *comeliness*, which up until then was lying *hidden*.

[MT II.2]

As I see it, however, we should praise the removal [of attributes] in a way that is contrary to the attributions. For we used to make assertions by beginning from the first and going down through intermediaries to the lowest things. Here, on the other hand, making ascent from the lowest to the more primordial, and [passing] through intermediaries back to the farthest, we remove all things in order that we may know without veil that ignorance, which is veiled around by all knowable things in all existents, and that we may see that darkness beyond being hidden by all the light in existing things.

[Gloss]
[10] *Oportet autem*, etc. ["As I see it, however"], down to the end of the chapter: this is the meaning.

In the foregoing books I have praised God through affirmations. In this one, however, we should give praise through negations and the removal of all things, in (as it were) the contrary way. For there, beginning with the affirmation or positing of the more primordial realities, we made our descent *through the intermediaries to the lowest*; *here, on the other hand*, beginning with the removal *of the lowest things* we ascend right up to the removal of the *more primordial realities*, step by step through the intermediaries. And when we are turned back once again to the farthest, equally *we take away* all things from it. The reason why we do this is in order *to know*, without the veil of mystical signification, the divine incomprehensibility hiding under the mystical veils *of all existing things* that can be known or thought by us. We do this, moreover, in order to contemplate the divine incomprehensibility, which exceeds all being. This indeed *is hidden* from all the knowledge in all creatures.

Capitulum tertium

[11] Titulus huius capituli est "Quae sunt catafatice, id est affirmative theologie, et que sunt apofatice, id est negative." In tribus enim voluminibus sive libris egit beatus Dyonisius de cataphatica, id est affirmativa theologia: in libro "de ypotiposibus,"[33] in quo agit de distinctionibus personarum; in secundo "de divinis nominibus"; in tertio "de vocabulorum transsumpcionibus ad divina designanda"; in quarto autem libro, id est "mystica theologia," specialiter agit de apophatica, id est negativa quae scilicet omnia a Deo removet tam inferiora quam media et superiora, ut videlicet per remocionem universalem a Deo ipsum Deum tandem inveniat singularem.

[MT III.1]

Igitur in theologicis hypotyposibus maxime propria affirmative theologie laudavimus: quomodo divina et bona natura singularis dicitur, quomodo trina; que secundum ipsam dicta paternitas et filiatio, quid vult monstrare spiritus theologia; quomodo ex immateriali et simplici bono in corde manentia bonitatis pullulaverunt lumina; et quomodo a mansione in ipso et in se ipsis et in se invicem coeterna pullulatione permanserunt inegressibilia; quomodo supersubstantialis Iesus humane nature veritatibus substantia factus est; et quecumque alia ab eloquiis expressa in theologicis hypotyposibus laudantur. In libro autem de divinis nominibus, quomodo bonus nominatur, quomodo exsistens, quomodo vita et sapientia et virtus, et quecumque alia intelligibilis sunt deinominationis. In symbolica autem theologia, que sunt a sensibilibus ad divina deinominationes, que sunt divine forme, que figure divine et partes et instrumenta, que divina loca et qui ornatus, et qui furores, que tristitie et insanie, que ebrietates et crapule, que iuramenta et que maledictiones, qui somni et que vigilationes, et quecumque alie sancte formationes composite sunt symbolice deiformationes.

---

[33] ypotiposibus MZVD] ypothesibus B

Chapter III
[Title and summary]
[11] The title of this chapter is, "What belongs to cataphatic, that is, affirmative, theology and what to apophatic, that is, negative." For Bl. Dionysius discussed the cataphatic or affirmative theology in three volumes or books: in the book *Theological Representations*, in which he treats of the distinctions of [the divine] persons; in the second,
Divine Names; in the third, *Verbal Metaphors Designating Divine Things*. In the fourth
book, on the other hand, that is, *Mystical Theology*, he treats especially of apophatic, that
is negative [theology]. This is the one which removes all things from God, lower things
as much as intermediary and higher things, with the aim, of course, that by the universal removing [of things] from God he may in the end find God alone.

[MT III.1]

In the *Theological Representations*, therefore, we praised the expressions
which are most appropriate to affirmative theology: how the divine and
good nature is called unique, how it is called threefold; what within it is
called fatherhood and sonship, what the theology of the Spirit wishes to
show; how from the immaterial and simple Good the lights remaining in
the heart of the Good sprouted, and in that co-eternal sprouting have
remained without departing from their dwelling in it, as well as in themselves and in each other. And how Jesus, who is beyond particular being,
has become a being in the true qualities of human nature, and whatever
other things, expressed in the Scriptures, are praised in the *Theological Representations*. In the book on the *Divine Names*, on the other hand, in what
sense he is called good, in what sense existing, life, wisdom and power, and
whatever other things belong to the intelligible naming of God. But in the
Symbolic Theology, what names of God are taken from the things of sense
in the direction of the divine things of God; what the divine forms are;
the figures, and the parts and the organs; what the divine places are and
what the ornaments; what are the angers, griefs and rage; how is he said
to be drunk, and sick with it; and about his oaths and curses; what are his
sleepings and wakings, and indeed the other divinely-formed representations which belong to the description of God through symbols.

[12] *Igitur in theologiciis* usque ad illud *Et te arbitror,* talis est sensus.

In tractatu "de divinis caracteribus," id est personalibus distinctionibus, *maxime* affir-macionibus usi sumus sive posicionibus in divinis laudibus, ubi ostendimus quod *divina* natura *singularis* est in essentia et trina in personis, et qualiter intelligenda est in Deo *paternitas et filiacio*, et quid significet proprietas quam sacra scriptura attribuit *Spiritui* Sancto, id est processio, iuxta illud, *Spiritum veritatis qui a Patre procedit* [Jn 15:26]. Item quomodo plenitudo bonorum invisibilium que fixe manet in corde Patris, *pululat ex immateriali et simplici bono*, id est persona Patris a qua procedit persona Filii per gen-eracionem et persona Spiritus Sancti per processionem, quorum uterque a Patre accepit[34] eandem plenitudinem, et per hoc Filius et Spiritus Sanctus manent in Patre et in se ipsis et omnes tres in se invicem, et ipsa luminum plenitudo in Filio et Spiritu per-manet coeterne Patri a quo uterque ipsorum originem habet, que tamen nihilominus tota manet in Patre. In eodem etiam libro tractavimus quomodo *Iesus*, qui est *super-substancialis* secundum deitatem, *factus est* homo secundum veram humanitatem, et alia multa ibi tractavimus iuxta *expressa* scripture testimonia. *In libro autem "de divinis nominibus"* tractavimus *quomodo* Deus dicitur bonus, *quomodo existens, quomodo vita et sapiencia*, et de aliis intelligibilibus Dei nominibus. *In "symbolica" autem theologia* trac-tavimus transumpciones vocabulorum rerum sensibilium ad designandum anagogice invisibilia divina, monstrando videlicet quomodo accipiendum sit quod Deo[35] attribu-untur *forme*, ut illud: *qui cum in forma Dei esset* [Phil 2:6]; *figure*, ut illud Ose: *quasi leena* [Os 13:7]; aut *partes*, ut illud cantici, *caput eius aurumque*[36] [Cant 5:11]; aut *instrumenta*, ut illud Amos: *trulla cementarii* [Am 7:7]; aut *loca*, ut illud Ezechielis: *benedicta gloria domini de loco isto* [Ez 3:12]; aut *ornatus*, ut illud Apocalypsis: *vestitum podere*[37] [Apoc 1:13]; aut *furores*, ut illud: *Domine, ne in furore* [Ps 6:1]; aut *tristicie*, ut illud: *tristis est anima mea* [Mt 26:38; Mk 14:34]; aut *insanie*, ut illud Osee: *scitote te Israhel stultum prophetam insanum* [Os 9:7]; aut *ebrietates et crapule*, psalmus: *tamquam potens crapulatus a vino* [Ps 77:65]; aut *iuramenta*, ut illud: *juravit dominus* [Ps 109:4]; aut *maledicciones*, ut illud: *maledicta terra in opere tuo*; [Gn 3:17]; aut *sumpnia*, ut illud, *exurge, quare obdormis?* [Ps 43:23]; aut *evigilaciones*, ut illud: *cor meum vigilat* [Cant 5:2]. Nec solum de istis ibi tractavimus, sed et de aliis compositis formacionibus Deo attributis, in libro *de symbolica theologia.*

---

[34] a patre accepit] accipit a patre B
[35] deo] *om.* B
[36] aurumque] optimum *add.* B
[37] podere] pondere MSS

[Gloss]
[12] *Igitur in theologicis*, etc. ["In the *Theological Representations*"] down to *Et te arbitror*, etc. ["I think you have been able"]: this is the meaning.

In the tract *On the Divine Characters*, that is, the distinctions of the persons, we have made *maximal* use of affirmations or assertions in the divine praises, where we show that the *divine* nature is *unique* in essence and three in persons. Also how *fatherhood and sonship* are to be understood in God, and what the property may signify which sacred Scripture attributes to the Holy *Spirit*, that is, procession, according to the text: *The Spirit of truth who proceeds from the Father*. Again, how the fullness of invisible goods, which remains fixed in the heart of the Father, *sprouts from the immaterial and simple good*, that is, the person of the Father, from whom the person of the Son proceeds through generation and the person of the Holy Spirit through procession. Each of the others has received from the Father the same fullness, and in this way the Son and the Holy Spirit remain in the Father and in themselves, and all three in each other. And the fullness of lights in the Son and the Spirit remains co-eternal with the Father from whom each of the other persons originates. The fullness remains none the less complete in the Father. In the same book we have discussed how *Jesus*, who is *above particular being* according to deity, *was made* man in true humanity. And many other things we have treated there in line with the *express* testimonies of Scripture. *In the book on the Divine Names*, however, we have discussed *how* God is said to be good, *how* he is said to be *existing, life and wisdom*, and the other intelligible names of God. *In Symbolic Theology, on the other hand*, we have discussed the carryover of words and sensible things in order to designate anagogically the invisible divine things, showing, that is, how it is to be understood that *forms* are attributed to God, as in this text: *Who, when he was in the form of God*; *figures*, Osee: *like a lioness*; or *parts*, Canticle: *His head is the best gold*; or *instruments*, Amos: *the trowel of the mason*; *places*, as in Ezechiel: *Blessed the glory of God from this place*; or *ornaments*, Apocalypse: *dressed in a garment reaching to the heels*; or *anger*: *Lord, do not in your anger*; or *sadness*: *My soul is sad*; or *madness*, Osee: *Know Israel to be a stupid prophet and insane*; or *drunkenness and sickness following it*, Psalms: *Like a strong man sick with wine*, or *oaths*: *The Lord has sworn*; or *curses*: *cursed is the earth in his work*; or *sleep*: *Arise, why do you sleep?* or *waking*: *My heart keeps vigil*. It is not only of these that we have treated there but also of other composite images attributed to God in the book, *Symbolical Theology*.

[MT III.2]

Et te arbitror conspexisse quomodo plurium sermonum sunt ultima quam prima. Etenim oportebat theologicas hypotyposes et divinorum nominum reserationem pauciorum sermonum esse quam symbolicam theologiam; quoniam quantum superius respicimus tantum sermones conspectibus intelligibilium contrahuntur. Quemadmodum et nunc et caliginem que est super mentem introeuntes, non sermonum brevitatem sed irrationabilitatem perfectam et imprudentiam inveniemus. Et ibi quidem a superiori ad extrema descendens, sermo secundum quantitatem descensus ad proportionalem dilatabatur multitudinem; nunc autem ab inferioribus ad supremum ascendens secundum mensuram ascensionis contrahitur; et post omnem ascensionem totus sine voce erit, totus unietur ineffabili. Dicis autem: quare totaliter a primo ponentes divinas positiones, ab ultimis inchoamus divinam ablationem? Quoniam hoc quod est super omnem positionem ponentes, a magis ipsi cognato suppositivam affirmationem oportebat ponere; illud autem quod est super omnem ablationem auferentes, a magis distantibus ab ipso auferre. An non magis est vita et bonitas quam aer et lapis? et magis non est crapula et non insania quam non dicitur neque intelligitur?

[13] *Et te arbitror* etc., usque in finem capituli, talis est sensus.

Ego puto quod tu, Thimothee, oculis mentis perspexeris quomodo tractatus nostri[38] *ultimi* plus habundant in verbis *quam primi*. Erat enim necesse quod libri "de divinis caracteribus" vel personalibus distinctionibus et "de divinis nominibus" minus essent in verbis prolixiores quam fuerit "symbolice theologie tractatus." Et racio ista est quoniam

---

[38] nostri] mei B

[MT III.2]

I think you have been able to see how it is that the last things are expressed in more words than the first. For it was necessary that the *Theological Representations* and the disclosure of the *Divine Names* should be briefer than the *Symbolic Theology.* The reason is, that the more we look to the higher the more the words are contracted by our glances at the intelligible things. So that now as we enter into the darkness which is beyond the mind we shall find not brevity in words but perfect irrationality and unwisdom. In the other case, indeed, the discourse went downward from the highest things to the lowest, and it was widened out to an extent proportional to the quantity of descent. At present, ascending from the lower things to the highest, it is contracted according to the measure of the ascent. And after the whole ascent [the discourse] will be completely voiceless, and will be united wholly to the One who is beyond discourse. But you say: why should we have started from the absolutely first when laying down positive statements about the divine? Why do we make the taking away [of attributes] from the divine begin from the lowest? The reason is that because [the First] is beyond every assertion, those who are making an affirmation that is more than affirmation, had to base the assertion on what is more cognate to the First. When we are removing that which is above all removal it was necessary to make the removal [of attributes] from him starting from the more distant things. Or is he not rather life and goodness than air and stone? And is he not further from being sickness and madness than from not lying within speech and understanding?

[Gloss]
[13] *Et te arbitror,* etc. ["I think that you"], down to the end of the chapter: this is the sense.

I think that you, Timothy, may have perceived with the eyes of the mind how our *last* discussions abound *more* in words *than our first.* It was indeed necessary that the books *Theological Representations* (or *Personal Distinctions*), and *Divine Names* should be less verbally prolix than the discussion of *Symbolic Theology.* And the reason for that is, that the more the matter being discussed is high and removed from the sense, or

quanto materia de qua agitur est alcior et a sensu remocior aut ab imaginacione long-
inquior, tanto minus utendum est verbis sensibilibus et magis est exercendus oculus
intellectualis, propter quod in presenti libro ubi fit mencio de divina *caligine*, id est
incomprehensibilitate, que excedit omnem mentem tam humanam quam angelicam vel
que est super verbum intellectuale, non solum invenimus verborum *brevitatem* sed *per-
fectum* et incomparabilem excessum racionis ad investigandum et prudencie ad digne elo-
quendum.[39] In predictis etiam libris tractatus noster *a superioribus* ad inferiora *descendens* secundum maiorem vel minorem[40] descensum *dilatabitur*[41] ad maiorem vel
minorem prolixitatem.[42] Quasi diceret: quanto tractabam inferiora et sensibus propinquiora tanto magis habundabat verborum copia proporcionalis eidem sensui;[43] in presenti autem tractatu *ab inferioribus* ad superiora *conscendens*[44] *secundum mensuram ascensionis contrahitur* et coartatur. Cum autem ad mentis excessum[45] perventum fuerit, tunc
deficiet omnis sermo tam oris quam mentis, quia videlicet sermo mentis ineffabilem
Deum non loquitur, nec restat menti nisi ut tota et totaliter *ineffabili* et eterno verbo
uniatur. Cum enim inter mentem et deum nihil sit medium,[46] postquam[47] facta est
omnium a Deo remocio nihil restat nisi ad ipsum[48] supermentalis unicio. Queris autem
fortassis quae sit racio quare *posiciones* incipimus a dignioribus et *ablaciones* ab inferioribus. Cuius rei racio hec est, quia quando volumus per posicionem designare Deum
qui est super *omnem posicionem*, convenit ut ipsa digniora et magis ei propinqua principalius attribuamus eidem; quando vero volumus ipsum designare per *ablacionem*,
primo convenit illa ab eo auferre que *magis ab ipso distare* videntur. Verbi gratia, con-
gruencius et propinquius attribuitur ei *vita et bonitas* quam *aer vel lapis*. Et similiter evi-
dentius ab eo removetur[49] *crapula* et[50] *insania* quam *dici* vel *intelligi*.

---

[39] eloquendum] loquendum B
[40] maiorem vel minorem] maiorem et minorem B; vel maiorem vel minorem M
[41] dilatabitur] dilatatur B
[42] prolixitatem] prolixitate B
[43] sensui] descensui B
[44] conscendens] ascendens B
[45] excessum] accessum B
[46] Cf. St. Augustine, *De lib. arb.* I.10.21; *De 83 quaest.* 54; *De vera rel.* 55.113; *De Gen. lib. imperf.* 16.60;
Enarr. in Ps. 118. 18.4.
[47] postquam] post B
[48] ad ipsum] *om.* B
[49] ab eo removetur] removetur ab eo B
[50] et] vel B

further from the imagination, the less must words belonging to the senses be used and the more should the intellectual eye be exercised. On that account we find in the present book not only *brevity* of words but a *perfect* and incomparable ecstasy of reason in relation to inquiry and of wisdom regarding worthy speech, where mention is made of the divine *darkness*, that is, the incomprehensibility which transcends every mind whether human or angelic, or which is beyond the intellectual word. In the books referred to, also, our discussion *descends from higher things* to lower; according to the greater or lesser descent *it will be broadened out* to a greater or lesser prolixity. As though he meant: for as long as I was discussing things lower and closer to the senses the more the supply of words abounded proportionately to the senses. In the present treatise, on the other hand, *mounting up from lower* to higher, *as we go up* the [supply of words] *is contracted* and narrowed. But when we reach the ecstasy of the mind, at that point all discourse, whether of mouth or of mind, will fail, because of course the discourse of the mind does not speak the God beyond discourse. It remains only for the mind *to be united* whole and wholly *to the ineffable* and eternal Word. For since there is no intermediary between the mind and God, after the removal of all [attributes] from God is done there remains nothing but uniting beyond the mind. But perhaps you ask what the reason is why we begin *the positive attributions* from the more worthy things and *the removals* [of attributes] from the lower. This is the reason: when we wish to designate the God above *all assertion*, by asserting something, it is fitting that we attribute more primordially to him the things of greater dignity, things that are closer to him. When, on the other hand, we wish to designate him through *removal*, it is fitting to remove from him first those things which seem to be *rather distant from him*, for example: *life and goodness* are more fittingly attributed to him and are closer to him than *air or stone*. And similarly it is more evident to remove from him *sickness* and *madness* than [the ability] *to be expressed in speech* or *in understanding*.

Capitulum quartum

[14] Titulus huius capituli est "Quod nihil est sensibilium omnis sensibilis per excellentiam causalis." Deus enim, qui est *causa* causalissima *omnium*, merito nihil esse dicitur sensibilium, sive activum sit sive[51] passivum. Et ideo beatus Dyonisius, ostendere volens excellenciam huius causae, primo ab ea removet remociora, ut est non substanciatum, ut non ens et non vivens ut lapis, et non rationale ut pecus. Et notantur hic tres gradus inferiores creature[52] quos removet, videlicet eorum que tantum sunt et non vivunt, item eorum que sunt et que vivunt sed non senciunt; item eorum que vivunt et senciunt sed non racionantur nec intelligunt; postremo removet omnia quae possunt corpori vel sensibus subiacere.

[MT IV.1]

Dicimus igitur quod omnium causa, et super omnia exsistens, neque sine [omitted, T.G.] substantia est neque sine [omitted, T.G.] vita, neque sine ratione [neque ratio, T.G.] neque sine mente [neque mens, T.G.]; neque corpus est, neque figura neque forma, neque qualitatem aut quantitatem aut pondus habet; neque in loco est neque videtur; neque tactum sensibilem habet, neque sentitur neque sensibilis est; neque inordinationem habet neque perturbationem a passionibus materialibus perturbata; neque impotens est, sensibilibus subiecta casibus; neque in indigentia est luminis; neque variationem aut corruptionem aut divisionem aut privationem aut passionem aut fluxum aut aliquid aliud sensibilium neque habet neque est.

[15] *Dicimus igitur*, etc. usque ad finem capituli, talis est sensus.

Asserimus quod Deus, qui creavit omnia et est super omnia, inchoando in eo ablacionem, non est aliquid materialiter substanciatum sive ens,[53] nec vivens *nec racione* utens *nec mente* eminens. Hec autem omnia a se invicem sunt remota et a Deo, quia non-ens remocius est a Deo quam ea que sunt, et non-vivens quam ea que sunt et

---

[51] sive] vel M
[52] inferiores creature] inferiores B; inferioris creature Z
[53] ens] *om.* M

Chapter IV
[Title and summary]
[14] The title of this chapter is, "The cause of every sensible thing which is beyond cause, is not one of the sensible things." For God, who is the *most causal cause* of all things, is rightly said not to be one of the sensible things, whether active or passive. For that reason Bl. Dionysius, wishing to show forth the excellence of this cause, first removes from it the most remote things, for example, not made into a substance, not being, and not living, like the stone, and not rational, like the cattle. Let the three inferior grades of creature be noted here which he removes, that is to say, those which simply are but are not living; those which are and are living but are not sentient; those which are living and sentient but which neither reason nor understand. Finally, he removes all that can fall under the body or the senses.

[MT IV.1]

We say, therefore, that the cause of all things, existing beyond all, is neither a substance, nor life, nor reason, nor mind, nor body, nor shape, nor form; it has neither quality nor quantity or weight; it is not in place nor is it seen; it does not have sensible touch nor can it be felt, nor is it endowed with sense; it does not suffer from disorder or disturbance coming from the material passions, nor is it powerless nor subject to sensible events, nor is it in need of light, nor does it have variation or corruption or division or privation or passivity, or flux or any other sensible thing; nor is it any of these.

[Gloss]
[15] *Dicimus igitur*, etc. ["We say, therefore"] down to the end of the chapter: this is the sense.

We assert that God, who created all things, also is beyond all things. We do this by beginning the removal process in him: he is not some thing, material, by mode a substance or being, nor a living thing nor one employing reason, nor one who is eminent by his mind. All these things, however, are at a remove from each other and from God, because non-being is more remote from God than the things that are, and non-living than those which both are and live; and lacking reason and mind is more remote than those things which are and are living, and which reason and understand. After that let

vivunt, et carens racione et mente est hiis remocius[54] que sunt et vivunt, et raciocinantur et[55] intelliguntur. Deinde removemus ab eo omne corporeum et omnia corpori vel rei corporee accidencia, ut est *figura, forma, qualitas, quantitas, pondus, localitas,* sensuum proprietas tam activa quam passiva. Similiter ab eo auferimus *inordinacionem* a carnalibus concupiscenciis provenientem, et complecionem carnalis desiderii *a materialibus passionibus* perturbatam vel turbidam factam. Item removemus ab eo impotenciam vel invaletudinem subiectam casibus sensibilibus. Item removemus ab eo *luminis indigentiam,* et *variacionem* vel generacionem et *corrupcionem,* et *divisionem,* cum non sit ex diversis compositus. Similiter passibilitatem materialem et *fluxum* temporalem ab eo auferimus cum non sit aliquid istorum aut in se habeat; nec sit aliquid sensibilium.

Capitulum quintum

[16] Titulus capituli huius est "Quod nihil est intelligibilium omnis intelligibilis per excellentiam causalis." Sicut enim a causa causalissima removentur sensibilia ita et intelligibilia, cum ipsa non sit sensibilis nec intelligibilis cuiuscumque dignitatis sit illud sensibile vel intelligibile quod illi cause[56] sit attribuibile. Hanc autem inter creaturam et creatorem[57] distanciam non est dubium operari summe cause[58] excellentiam, quae sicut in se est ineffabilis, ita nulli a se causato[59] est comparabilis. Unde quoniam nulla esse potest ibi comparatio congrua, ibi cadit tam in sensibilibus quam in intelligibilibus remocio.

[MT V.1]

Rursus autem ascendentes dicimus quod neque anima est neque mens; neque phantasiam aut opinionem aut rationem aut intellectum habet; neque ratio est neque intellectus; neque dicitur neque intelligitur; neque numerus est neque ordo; neque magnitudo neque parvitas; neque equalitas; neque inequalitas;[60] neque similitudo neque dissimilitudo; neque stat

---

[54] est hiis remocius] remocius est ab hiis B
[55] et raciocinantur et] nec raciocinantur nec B
[56] cause] *om.* B
[57] creaturam et creatorem] creatorem et creaturam B
[58] summe cause] sine me M
[59] nulli a se causato] nullo a se causato M; nullo causato a se B
[60] neque inequalitas] *om.* Z

us remove from him everything corporeal, and all accidents of a body or a bodily thing, such as *shape, form, quality, quantity, weight, location,* property (whether active or passive) of the senses. Similarly, we take away from him *disorder* coming *from the carnal concupiscences*; also being overtaken by a carnal desire disturbed or troubled by material passions. Again, we remove from him powerlessness or inability that is subject to sensible events. Again, we shall remove from him *the want of light,* and *variation* (or generation), *and corruption* and *division,* since he is not composed of different things. In a similar way we take away material passivity and temporal *flux,* since he is not one of those things nor does he have them in himself; nor is he any one of the sensible things.

Chapter V
[Title and summary]
[16] The title of this chapter is, "That the transcendent cause of every intelligible reality is not one of the intelligible realities." Just as sensible things are removed from the most causal cause, so also are intelligible things, since it is neither sensible nor intelligible, whatever the degree of dignity that sensible or intelligible thing might possess which could be attributed to that cause. But there is no doubt that this distance between the creature and the creator brings about the transcendence of the highest cause, which, just as in itself it is beyond discourse, so it is comparable to nothing created by it. Since, then, there can be no comparison in that case, a suitable removal comes in, regarding both sensible things and intelligible.

[MT V.1]

As we ascend again we say that it is not soul nor mind; nor has it imagination or opinion, nor reason or intellect — it is not reason or intellect; it is not spoken, it is not understood; it is not number or order, nor greatness or smallness, nor equality or inequality; nor similarity or dissimilarity; it neither stays at rest nor is moved; nor does it bring about silence or have power; nor is it power or light; it does not live nor is it life; it is not substance, nor everlastingness nor time; it cannot be grasped by the understanding; it is not knowledge or truth; nor kingship nor wisdom; it is neither one nor oneness, nor deity nor goodness. It is not a spirit in the sense that we understand that, nor sonship nor fatherhood, nor anything that is understood by us or by any other being; nor is it anything among non-

neque movetur, neque silentium agit; neque virtutem habet neque virtus est; neque lumen neque vita est neque vivit; neque substantia est; neque evum neque tempus; neque tactus est eius intelligibilis neque scientia; neque veritas neque regnum neque sapientia; neque unum neque unitas; neque deitas aut bonitas; neque spiritus est sicut nos videmus, neque filiatio neque paternitas; neque aliquid aliud cognitum a nobis aut ab alio quodam exsistentium; neque est aliquid exsistentium neque aliquid non exsistentium est; neque ipsam cognoscunt exsistentia secundum quod ipsa est; neque ipsa cognoscit ea que sunt exsistentia secundum quod exsistentia sunt; neque ratio ipsius est neque nomen neque cognitio est; neque tenebre neque lumen; neque error neque veritas; neque est ipsius universaliter positio neque ablatio; sed eorum que sunt post ipsam positiones et ablationes facientes, ipsam neque ponimus neque auferimus; quoniam et super omnem positionem est perfecta et unitiva omnium causa, et super omnem ablationem est excessus ab omnibus simpliciter absoluti et super tota.

[17] *Rursus autem*, etc. usque in finem capituli talis est sensus.

Inchoantes denuo negaciones ab altioribus divinis, *dicimus quod Deus*, qui est omnium causa, *neque anima est*, quia corpus non vivificat, *neque mens*, quia non supereminet anime ut superior pars anime, *nec fantasiam*[61] habet divina vel spiritalia ymaginando, nec *opinionem* in diversas sentencias diversimode declinando, nec *racionem* inter dubia discernendo, nec *intellectum habet* circa solum creata visibilia insistendo, *neque est racio* inter bonum et malum discernens, *nec intellectus* circa invisibilia creata insistens, *neque dicitur* quia non est effabilis, *neque intelligitur* quia a nullo est comprehensibilis.

Ut autem decurramus per media ad extrema rursus dicimus, quod *neque numerus* est quia non est multiplicabilis, *neque ordo* quia non est ad paria vel inparia proporcionabilis,[62] *neque magnitudo* quia non est augmentabilis, *neque parvitas* quia non est minorabilis, *neque equalitas* quia non est proporcionabilis, *neque similitudo* quia nulli rei est comparabilis, *neque dissimilitudo* qui a nulla re est discrepabilis; *neque stat* quia non

---

[61] fantasiam] fantasia B
[62] quia non est ad paria vel inparia] quia non ad paria vel inparia non est BM

existents or among existents; nor do existents know it as it itself is; nor does it know existing things as such; there is no expression of it nor name nor knowledge; it is not darkness and it is not light, it is not error and it is not truth; it is completely beyond any positive attribution or removal; while we make attributions or removals [of attributes] from those things that come after it, we neither assert nor remove anything concerning it, since beyond every assertion it is the perfect and uniting cause of all things, and it transcends] all removal by virtue of its simple and absolute nature beyond all things.

[Gloss]
[17] *Rursus autem*, etc. ["As we ascend again"] down to the end of the chapter: this is the meaning.

Beginning at last the negations from the higher, divine things, *we say that God*, who is the cause of all things, *is not soul*, because he does not vivify a body; *nor mind*, because he does not stay above the soul as its higher part; *nor* has he *imagination*, imagining divine or spiritual things; nor *opinion*, inclining in different ways to different proposi-tions; nor *reason*, discriminating between doubts; *nor does he have understanding* apply-ing itself to created, visible things alone; *nor is he reason*, discerning between good and bad; *nor intellect*, applying itself to created, invisible things, *nor is he spoken*, for he is not speakable; *nor is he understood*, for he is not comprehensible by anyone.

But to run downward through the intermediaries to the last, we say again that he is *not number*, because he is not multipliable; *nor order*, because he is not proportionate to even or uneven; *nor greatness*, because he is not subject to increase; *nor smallness*, because he is not subject to reduction; *nor equality*, because he cannot be proportioned; *nor similarity*, because he is not comparable to any thing; *nor dissimilarity*, because he is not discrepant from anything; *nor does he stay at rest*, because he is not an immobile thing; *nor is he moved*, because he is not a thing that rolls; *nor does he bring silence*, because he cannot be confined to a mental or vocal word.

est res immobilis; *neque movetur* quia non est volubilis; *neque silencium agit*, quia non est verbo mentali vel vocali repressibilis.[63]

Ut autem ad summa per quaedam media revertamur et in summis creaturis negaciones terminemus, dicimus quod *nec virtutem habet* qua ab alio solidetur; *neque virtus est* qua ab alio informetur; *neque lumen* est quod ab alio mutuetur; *neque vivit* ut ab alio sensificetur; neque vita est ad regendum aliquod corpus accomodatum;[64] *neque substantia est* materialiter substantiatus; *neque evum* quia non est spatium invariabile, *nec tempus* quia non est spacium mutabile. *Nec* est *tactus*, quia secundum essenciam suam[65] non est aliqualiter tangibilis; nec est *sciencia* quia non est cognoscibilis; *neque veritas* quia non est intellectui equabilis; *neque regnum* quia non est dominabilis; *neque sapiencia* quia non est gustabilis; *neque unum* quia non est in plura augmentabilis, *neque unitas* quia non est materialiter indivisibilis; *neque* est *deitas* a nobis intelligibilis; neque *bonitas* quia non est qualitas infusibilis; *neque spiritus est* a nobis intelligibilis; *neque filiacio* ab alio secundum nos generabilis; neque *paternitas* alterius subsistentis materialiter productibilis; *neque* est *aliud cognitum a nobis* plene, vel ab aliquo existente scilicet homine vel angelo; *neque est aliquid non existencium* intellectualiter, neque aliquid existencium materialiter; *neque existentia ipsum cognoscunt secundum quod ipse est, nec ipse cognoscit* ea[66] secundum quod ipsa existunt in se ipsis sed secundum quod sunt in verbo. Item nec est[67] ipsius racionalis investigacio nec nominis imposicio, nec cognicionis conprehensio; nec est *tenebre* a lumine deficientes, nec est *lumen* intelligibile; *neque est error* quo animus decipiatur *nec veritas* qua[68] sua industria animus illustratur. Et omnino nulla est eius *positio* vel *ablacio*, sed cum quecumque alia de ipso ponimus vel ab ipso auferimus, *ipsum tamen* nunquam *ponimus vel auferimus, quoniam et super omnem posicionem est perfecta omnium causa*, et *super omnem ablacionem est excessus* eius *ab omnibus* et super omnia absolutus.

Explicit exposicio super misticam theologiam (B)

Explicit mistica theologia. amen (M)

Explicit theologia mistica (Z)

Explicit opus multum utile, et obscurum valde. (V)

---

[63] repressibilis] reprehensibilis B
[64] accomodatum] accomodatus B
[65] suam] *om.* M
[66] ea] *om.* B
[67] est] *om.* B
[68] qua] que B

However, to return to the highest things through some intermediaries, and to end the negations among the highest creatures: we say that *he neither has power*, in which he may be established by another; *nor is he power*, in which he may be informed by another; *nor is he light*, which is procured by another; *nor is he living*, to be given sense by another; nor is he life, adapted to rule some body. *Nor is he substance*, materially made substance; *nor is he eternity*, because he is not an invariable stretch; *nor time*, because he is not a mutable stretch; *nor is he touch*, because in his essence he is not in any way touchable; nor is he *knowledge*, because he is not knowable; *nor truth*, because he cannot be equated with the intellect; *nor kingship*, because he cannot be made into a ruler; *nor wisdom*, because he cannot be savored; *nor one*, because he cannot be increased to many; *nor unity*, because he is not materially indivisible; *nor* is he *deity*, intelligible to us; nor *goodness*, because he is not a quality that can be infused; *nor is he spirit*, to be understood by us; *nor sonship*, to be engendered by another in the way that we understand; nor *paternity*, which is able materially to produce another subsisting being; *nor is he anything thought*, totally *by us* or by any existent — man or angel; *nor is he anything among non-existents* in terms of intellect; nor anything of existent things in terms of matter; *nor do existents know him as he himself is; nor does he know them* as they are in themselves, but as they are in the Word. Furthermore, there is no rational inquiry into him, nor any giving of a name, nor comprehension of knowledge; nor is he *darkness* through the lack of light; nor is he intelligible *light*; *he is not error*, through which the mind is deceived; *nor truth*, by whose agency the mind is illuminated. And there is no *positive attribution* or *removal* of any kind in his regard. *But as we make positive attributions or remove other attributes from him we never either affirm or remove him, since the perfect cause of all things is beyond every attribution*, and his universal *transcendence lies beyond all removal of attributes*, since he is absolute, above all that there is.

PART II:
THE TRANSLATION AND COMMENTARY BY
ROBERT GROSSETESTE

1. Introduction

Robert Grosseteste, Bishop of Lincoln

Robert Grosseteste (before ca. 1168–1253) made an outstanding contribution to the thought and the culture of his time. The generation which witnessed the chartering of the universities of Paris and Oxford was full of a sense of vigorous scholastic renewal and intellectual innovation. Grosseteste made a distinctive contribution to the University of Oxford, the earliest years of which (1214–1235) he may fairly be said to have dominated, intellectually speaking. His life was full of initiatives of the most varied kind, which, when we take them all together, can be seen to have resulted in an exceptionally diversified output of writing: philosophical and scientific treatises; commentaries on Aristotle; biblical exegesis and theological reflection; letters and, not the least in importance, translations from the Greek. During his years as bishop of Lincoln, from 1235 up to his death, he continued to pursue his translating activities, while adding considerably to his output of sermons and pastoral writings and framing an influential set of constitutions for the Diocese of Lincoln.[1]

Authenticity

The authenticity of the translation and commentary by Grosseteste on the MT is guaranteed by its place within his studies of the four writings by that mysterious, Greek-language Christian author known as the Pseudo-Dionysius (fl. ca. 500). This considerable body of work was attributed to *Lincolniensis* in several manuscripts, as well as by Roger Bacon. The ascription to Grosseteste of the new version of the four writings and of the commentary can be made quite firmly.

---

[1] The most recent general study of Grosseteste is: James McEvoy, *Robert Grosseteste*, Great Medieval Thinkers (New York: Oxford University Press, 2000).

Date of Composition

Can Grosseteste's work regarding MT be dated with precision? He himself (unlike Gallus) did not give any indication of its time of composition, but a discussion of the matter conducted over fifty years ago (but which could scarcely be bettered even at the present time) placed Grosseteste's concentrated work on the Pseudo-Dionysian writings in the years 1240–1243.[2] The commentaries followed each other over two or three years, and MT was the last, after the *Celestial Hierarchy*, the *Ecclesiastical Hierarchy*, and the *Divine Names*. Grosseteste believed that this was the order in which the four works should be studied.

Greek Studies

It was as a translator from the Greek that Grosseteste was to achieve celebrity on the European scale. His Greek studies belonged to the second half of his long and productive life. It was only when he became bishop and had extra resources at his disposal that he began actually to translate, as distinct from reading, Greek authors. He learned Greek by using a grammar and a Byzantine etymological compilation (*Etymologicum Gudianum*) and encyclopedia (the so-called *Suda*). He may have had a teacher. In most cases he did not begin from nothing to translate but worked from already existing Latin versions. This is true of his work on writings by John of Damascus and on the *Ethics* of Aristotle. It also holds true of his version of Pseudo-Dionysius: as he worked he had before him the translations of Eriugena and Sarrazen. He valued uniformity of translation, and it appears that he mentally assigned to each Greek term a Latin equivalent from which he did not often depart. His aim generally was to produce versions for serious study, not simply for reading through. In other words, he opted for a style of translating that mirrored the Greek articulation of meaning. The Latin he deployed was the faithful vehicle of the Greek original. He preferred to accompany his versions by a commentary or extensive glosses, many of these defending his choice of words in the translation itself, as the necessary complement to the study of the latter.

---

[2] See Daniel A. Callus, O.P., "The Date of Grosseteste's …," pp. 186–209.

Translation of Pseudo-Dionysius, and Commentary

The Greek text from which Grosseteste re-translated the four writings survives as *Bodleian MS Can. gr. 97*. It was produced at Paris specially for his use. It includes variant readings from three Greek manuscripts, and also the scholia attributed globally to St. Maximus Confessor, which Grosseteste also translated for the first three works; in his Greek manuscript the scholia on MT are missing (the reason for this is not evident), and in his commentary he does not refer to them. Each short section (or *particula*) of translated Greek was followed by a commentary. The translation and the exposition coming after it were joined in a unity that Grosseteste clearly wished to be indissoluble. He took up the text in gobbets and wove it into a more fluent discourse that ordered, clarified, magnified and diversified the wording of the version itself. He discussed the quality of the existing translations, and on occasion weighed up the Greek variants. He explained the difficult words in a passage, and tried to iron out ambiguities resulting from punctuation, or affecting the construction of the text. He regularly related the progress of the discussion immediately in hand to his author's discourse taken as a whole, reconciling apparent contradictions. He frequently ended by commending the thought of his author to the appreciation of his reader. He aimed at the total recovery, in Latin, of the sense of the original. These recurrent expository features and characteristics can all be identified in his commentary on MT.

Manuscripts and Editions

Upwards of twenty manuscripts preserve the text of the work that concerns us, some in the form of excerpts. The majority of them ascribes the work to Grosseteste. Since the latter's study of the other three writings by the same author is witnessed to by ten manuscripts (on average), it can be seen that the MT translation and commentary was frequently copied in isolation from the others. This was particularly the case in the fifteenth century. The work has been published twice as a whole. In 1502–1503 it was printed in Strasbourg in *Opera Dionysii*, which included the translation of Sarrazen and the version and commentary of Grosseteste (fols 264b–271b). The translation was printed in *Dionysiaca* I, 565–669, in the company of the other Latin translations ranging in time from Hilduin to Dom Joachim Périon. The version and commentary were published by Ulderico Gamba in Milan, in 1942.[3]

---

[3] See Bibliography.

The Edition

The credit for the pioneering study of the Greek-Latin translations of Robert Grosseteste belongs to Ezio Franceschini, sometime Rector of Sacro Cuore University, Milan. Ulderico Gamba seems to have been a pupil of his, and a worthy one at that: he produced an edition of the translation and commentary on MT that can lay a well-grounded claim to critical status.[4] It is based on four manuscripts of the thirteenth century, supported by the collation of four other witnesses and the Strasbourg edition, which has the same value as a manuscript. This edition has been reprinted in the present volume, with a small number of corrections. These consist of the insertion of an occasional word or phrase omitted in the existing edition. The MS. Dublin *Trinity College 164*, which was not available to Gamba, served as the basis for the verification of the text. The classical spelling used by him has been retained. The translated text has been printed in larger characters than the commentary, as Grosseteste probably wanted it done.

English Translation

The Latin version of Grosseteste has been turned into English, to help the reader use it in conjunction with the Latin translation and with the bishop's commentary. The result is rather literal. (Grosseteste would have approved!) Longer periods have often been broken up into several sentences. The gobbets of text have been italicized for identification within the commentary. Where Grosseteste attempted to reproduce for his reader the effect of a Greek composite term or other neologism of his author, the Latin word or phrase he uses has been retained but given an English translation in brackets. Biblical references have been placed in the Latin text of MT but have not been repeated in the commentary; those proper to the commentary are referenced within it. The Douay Bible, which was based directly upon the Vulgate, has been employed for quotations. Round brackets ( ) have been resorted to, to avoid ambiguity in the version of the commentary. Square brackets [ ] enclose words added by the translator.

---

[4] It seems that Gamba planned a complete study of the translations and commentaries on Pseudo-Dionysius from medieval times but was unable to complete the task. No detailed overall survey exists for this field.

2. *De Mystica Theologia*: the Version and Commentary by Robert Grosseteste (ca. 1242) — Latin Text

CONTINENTIE SINGULORUM LIBRORUM

Particularum primi capituli de mistica theologia continentie.

Prime continentia: Oratio auctoris ut attingat ad verticem mistice theologie, et quomodo pertingitur ad illum verticem.

Secunde: Quibus non sunt communicanda in priori particula pretacta.

Tertie: Quod omnium positiones et abnegationes dicuntur de Deo et non sunt de ipso opposite, et quomodo est multorum et paucorum et nullorum sermonum, et quod solum transcendentibus omnia et intrantibus caliginem fit manifestus.

Quarte: Ostensio graduum ascensionis in caliginem per factum a Moyse et circa Moysen.

Particularum secundi capituli continentie.

Prime continentia: Oratio quod attingat ad caliginem et in ea videat quoniam non contingit videre eum qui supra visionem, et laudet per omnium ablationem, cum exemplo facientis agalma.

Secunde: Quod contrariis viis incedit laus Dei per positiones et per ablationes et quod ea que est per ablationes magis ducit in caliginem.

Particularum tertii capituli continentie.

Prime continentia: Secundum que laudatur Deus in Theologicis Subfigurationibus et in libro De Divinis Nominibus et in Symbolica Theologia, et quod secundum illa laudatur positive.

Secunde: Quod extrema sunt multiloquiora primis, et secundum proportionem descensionis a primis ad extrema dilatatur et e converso abreviatur sermo, ita quod in caligine descendit et per abnegationes ascendit.

Duo ultima capitula non sunt secundum seriem littere in particulas divisa, quorum continentie sunt in titulis expresse.

3. English Translation

CONTENTS OF THE INDIVIDUAL BOOKS

Contents of the parts of the first chapter of *Mystical Theology*.

Content of the first part: Prayer of the author, to reach the peak of mystical theology, and how one gets there.

Of the second: Those to whom the former part is not to be communicated.

Of the third: That the assertions and denials of all things are said of God and are not opposites in relation to him; how he is of many words, and few, and none; and that he is made manifest only to those who transcend all and enter the darkness.

Of the fourth: Showing the steps of the ascent to the darkness through what Moses did; and concerning Moses.

Contents of the parts of the second chapter.

Content of the first: Prayer, that he may reach the darkness and may see in it that one does not arrive at seeing the one who is above vision; that he may praise through the taking away of all; with the example of someone making a statue.

Of the second: That the praise of God goes in contrary ways, through assertions and through taking away, and that the latter leads more to the darkness.

Contents of the parts of the third chapter.

Content of the first: In what respects God is praised in the *Theological Representations* and in the book on *Divine Names* and in *Symbolic Theology*; and that in these he is praised by affirmations.

Of the second: That the last are spoken of at greater length than the first; also, the discourse is drawn out and conversely it is shortened in proportion to the descent from the first things to the last, in such a way that it descends in darkness and ascends through the negations.

The last two chapters are not divided up into parts according to the order of the text; their contents are expressed in the titles.

[PREFATIO LINCOLNIENSIS]

Hec insunt in eo quod de mistica theologia capitula quinque.

primum: de mistica theologia.

secundum: qualiter oportet et uniri et ymnos reponere omnium cause et super omnia.

tertium: que affirmative theologie, que negative.

quartum: quoniam nihil sensibilium qui omnis sensibilis secundum superexcellentiam causa.

quintum: quoniam nihil intelligibilium qui omnis intelligibilis secundum superexcellentiam causa.

Dionisii areopagite episcopi athenarum ad Timotheum episcopum Ephesi De Mistica Theologia. compresbitero Timotheo Dionisius presbiter.

In nostris exemplaribus grecis non fuit prescriptum aliquod epigramma in hunc librum de mistica theologia. Aliqui tamen translatores ponunt epigramma verbis latinis sic:

> Novam claritatem in reliqua et scientiam subsistentium
> noctem per divinam, quam non iustum licet nominare.[1]

Vel sic:

> Et sensum refulgentem penetrasti et scientiam exsistentium
> noctem per divinam, quam non est fas nominare.[2]

Hoc epigramma non exponimus, quia ipsum grece scriptum non vidimus. Conicimus tamen quod diverse translationes, qua unus translator dixit: "novam claritatem" et alter, vel forte idem ex alio exemplari: "et sensum refulgentem," ex hoc habuerunt occasionem quod hec dictio *kainHn* significat novam, et, si scribatur *kai noyn*, significat "et intellectum" seu "et sensum." *Kai* enim, si superscribatur notula gravis accentus, significat "et," et *noyn* significat "intellectum" seu "sensum." Consimilis concidens scriptio occasio fuit huius diversitatis in: "reliqua" et "penetrasti." Hec autem diversitas "non iustum licet" et "non est fas," potest esse sola translationis eiusdem Greci diversitas. Evidens est autem quod noctem divinam vocat iste prescriptor eam, quam inferius dicit auctor caliginem in qua vere est Deus secundum eloquia.

---

[1] Eriugena's translation.
[2] Sarrazen's translation.

[PREFACE BY GROSSETESTE]

These five chapters are in the [discussion of] Mystical Theology:

First: On mystical theology.

Second: How it is necessary to be united to the cause of all and to give back praise.

Third: What belongs to affirmative theology and what to negative.

Fourth: The cause of every sensible thing which is beyond cause is nothing of the sensible things.

Fifth: That the transcendent cause of every intelligible reality is not one of the intelligible realities.

[Dedication]

From Dionysius the Areopagite, Bishop of Athens, to Timothy, Bishop of Ephesus, *On Mystical Theology*; to his fellow priest, Timothy, Dionysius the Priest.

[Note by Grosseteste]

In our Greek manuscripts there was no epigram written in front of this book *On Mystical Theology*. Yet some translators do have an epigram in Latin words, as follows:

> New brightness in the remainder and knowledge of things that exist,
> Through the divine night, which even to name would not be as it should.

Or thus:

> You have penetrated the shining sense and the knowledge of existing things
> Through the divine night, which it is not right to name.

We make no comment on this epigram because we have not seen it written in Greek. We conjecture, however, that the different translations, which in one case reads "a new brightness" and in another (or perhaps the same one but working from a different copy) "the shining sense," took their origin from the fact that the word *kainHn* means "new," and if it is written *kai noyn* means "and understanding," or even "sense." For if the sign for the grave accent is placed above *kai* it means "and"; *noyn* means "intellect" or "sense." A further similarity in the written word gave rise to the variation between "remainder" and "you have penetrated." On the other hand the difference between "it would not be as it should" and "it is not right" can be purely and simply a difference in translation of the same Greek expression. It is evident, however, that the divine night is the term used by the writer of the epigram for that "darkness" of which the author speaks in the book — the darkness in which God truly is, according to the Scriptures.

CAPITULUM PRIMUM

DIONISII AREOPAGITE DE MISTICA THEOLOGIA[3]

1. Trinitas supersubstantialis et superdea et superbona, eius que christianorum inspectrix divine sapientie, dirige nos ad misticorum eloquiorum superincognitum et superlucidum et supremum verticem, ubi simplicia et absoluta et invertibilia theologie misteria secundum superlucidam invelata sunt occulte docentis silencii caliginem, in tenebrosissimo supermanifestissimum superlustrantem, et in omnino intangibili et invisibili superpulcris claritatibus superimplentem inoculatos intellectus. Mihi quidem igitur hec orentur. Tu autem, o amice Timothee, ea que circa misticas visiones forti attricione et sensus derelinque et intellectuales operationes et omnia sensibilia et intelligibilia et omnia non entia et entia, et ad unionem, ut possibile, incognite restituere eius qui super omnem substantiam et cognitionem; ea enim, que tui ipsius et omnium irretentibili absoluta pure extasi, ad supersubstantialem divine tenebre radium, omnia auferens et ex omnibus absolutus, reduceris.

Mistica theologia est secretissima, et non iam per speculum [cf. I Cor 13:12] et per ymagines creaturarum cum Deo locutio, cum videlicet mens transcendit omnes creaturas et se ipsam, et otiatur ab actibus omnium virium apprehensivarum cuiuscumque creati, in desiderio videndi et tenendi ipsum qui super omnia, expectans in caligine privationis actualis comprehensionis, hoc est in caligine actualis ignorantie omnium, donec manifestet se desideratus, quantum novit convenire desiderantis dignitati et susceptibilitati. Dicitur autem misticum a *miω*, verbo greco quod significat "disco occulta" et "doceo occulta" seu "secreta," et "obscuro" et "constringo" et "claudo," unde mistica theologia dicitur quasi clausa et constricta: ea enim que dicta est, clausa est et constricta ab oculis omnium actu videntium aliquid creatum, et per hoc ab oculis omnium

---

[3] Grosseteste understood the chapter titles to be part of the work and so he translated them and used them in his commentary. In fact they were due to a Greek editor.

CHAPTER I

[Title] DIONYSIUS THE AREOPAGITE ON MYSTICAL THEOLOGY

1. Trinity beyond being, beyond divinity and goodness, guardian of Christians' divine wisdom! Show us the way towards that highest peak of mystical Scriptures exalted above unknowing and beyond brightness! There the simple, absolute, and changeless mysteries of the Word of God are covered in the brilliant darkness of a secretly-teaching silence, making the transcendent clarity shine (and more than shine!) in the darkest place, and completely filling sightless minds with the wholly unsensed and unseen brightness beyond all beauty. These things, therefore, are indeed requested by me. But you, Timothy my friend, by a mighty struggle regarding the mystical visions leave behind the operations of sense and intellect and all objects of sense and understanding, all that is and all that is not; and, without knowledge, strive upwards as much as you can, towards union with the One who is above all being and knowledge. For, removing all things and being freed from them all, by an irresistible and absolute ecstasy with regard to yourself and to all things, you will be uplifted to the ray of the divine shadows which is above all being.

[Commentary]

Mystical theology is the most secret talking with God, no longer through a mirror and through the images of creatures, but the kind where the mind transcends all creatures and itself, and relaxes from the acts of all the powers that are able to grasp anything created. In the desire of seeing and of holding him who is above all, the mind waits in the darkness of the privation of actual comprehension, that is, in the darkness of the actual unknowing of all things, until the one it desires may manifest himself — to the extent that he ever can correspond to the dignity and the receptivity of the one desiring. But the word "mystical" is taken from *miω*, a Greek verb which means "I learn hidden things" and "I teach hidden things" or secrets, and "I hide" and "I press together" and "I close." Whence theology is called "mystical" in the sense of "closed" and "constricted." For that theology which is referred to is closed and kept from the eyes of all who are actually seeing something created, and by that fact from the eyes of all common men actually living the present life. And it is moreover called "mystical" in the sense of

communium hominum vita actu viventium. Et dicitur insuper mistica quasi obscura, quia pretacta cum Deo locutio non habetur nisi in predicta ignorantie caligine. Dicitur etiam mistica quia occultissima et secretissima doctrina et disciplina edocta est et suscepta. Dicta itaque theologia, que est secretissima et occultissima cum Deo locutio et sermocinatio, proprie, principaliter et maxime dicitur mistica. Communius autem et minus proprie dicitur misticum omne spiritalius per minus spiritale vel per rem non spiritalem significatum, et misterium omne significans id quod est spiritalius; secretiora enim et occultiora et nobis obscuriora et clausa magis sunt spiritaliora et ideo cum per nobis manifestiora significantur et edocentur, dicuntur communiter mistica. Que autem ea nobis significant dicuntur misteria, quasi misticorum servativa et contentiva: derivatur enim misterium a *misticum* et *tHro* quod est "servo"; multi tamen abusive vocant misteria ea que dicuntur mistica.

Dicturus itaque auctor de theologia que proprie, principaliter et maxime dicitur mistica, invocat primo sanctissimam Trinitatem ut dirigat eum quousque mente transcenderit omnia et supremum attigerit verticem, ubi in caligine ignorantie sunt et suscipiuntur absque symbolis et ymaginibus divini radii superpulcre claritates. Si enim divina directione et manuductione ad hunc verticem attigerit, licet ibi visa et audita sint ineffabilia et que non licet homini loqui [II Cor 12:4], magis tamen et efficacius fari poterit de eorum ineffabilitate et de adaptatione ascensurorum et ascensu in illum verticem. Ait itaque: *Trinitas supersubstantialis et superdea et superbona*, excedit enim incomparabili et infinito excessu omne intelligibile per substantiam et per deitatem et per bonitatem; *Trinitas*, dico, inspectrix et inspectione datrix *eius divine sapientie que christianorum, dirige nos ad supremum verticem*, id est ad mentis excessum super omnem creaturam et super omnem actum virtutis apprehensive; verticem, dico, *misticorum eloquiorum*: in illo enim vertice, ut pretactum est, loquitur Deus cum homine et homo cum Deo secretissima illa locutione que est non per symbola nec ymagines, sed per ipsam non velatam visionem; *superincognitum*, quia illum non cognoscit nisi qui attingit, quod est rarissimorum, et quia in ipso est omnis cognitionis privatio actualis; *et superlucidum* quia in eo manifestat se lux que est super omnem lucem, sicut et quantum ipsa novit condecere sibi danti et convenire suscipienti; ubi, in quo vertice, *misteria theologie*, hoc est mistica et secretissima sermocinationis cum Deo (ibi enim idem est misterium et misticum, quia idem est significans et significatum, manifestans et manifestatum) *simplicia*, quia unico et simplici verbo loquitur Deus quecumque loquitur, et simplicissima mentis virtute auditur; *et absoluta*, quia sine simbolo et parabola; *et invertibilia*, quia immutabilem habent veritatem; ubi, inquam, misteria hec *invelata sunt*, id est abscondita sunt et cooperta ab oculis omnium secundum hominem viventium, *secundum caliginem superlucidam*,

"obscure," because the speaking with God referred to above does not occur except in the darkness of ignorance already mentioned. It is also called "mystical" because the most hidden and the most secret teaching and learning is taught and is received. And so this theology, which is the most secret and the most hidden speaking and talking with God, is called "mystical" in the proper sense, in the primary sense, and in the greatest sense. In a general and less literal way, however, "mystical" is used for everything more spiritual that is signified by the less spiritual, or by a reality that is not spiritual; and a mystery is everything which refers to something of a more spiritual nature. For the more secret and hidden things, and the things which are more obscure to us and more closed, are more spiritual, and therefore, since they are signified and taught by things that are more manifest to us, they are commonly called "mystical." But those realities that signify them for us are called "mysteries," since they (as it were) keep and contain the mystical things. For the word mystery is derived from *misticum* and *tHrω*, which means *servo*, "I keep." However, many quite wrongly use the term "mysteries" for those realities which are called "mystic."

And so the author, addressing himself to the theology which in the strict and principal and maximal sense is called mystical, first calls upon the most holy Trinity to direct him to the point where in his mind he shall have transcended all things and attained the highest peak, where, in the darkness of the unknowing of all things, the more-than-beautiful lights of the divine ray are, and are received, without symbols and images. For if by the divine guidance, and by being led by the hand, he should have reached this summit, even though the things there seen and heard are beyond speech, and are things which it is not right for man to speak, he will nevertheless be able to speak more, and more effectively, about their ineffability, and about the preparation of those who are going to make the ascent to that peak, and about the ascent itself. And so he says, *Trinity beyond being, beyond deity and goodness*, for it exceeds, by a transcendence beyond comparison, and infinitely, everything that can be understood by way of substance, deity and goodness. *Trinity*, I say, *guardian of that divine wisdom of Christians*, who by guarding grants it: *show us the way towards that highest peak*, that is, to where the mind transcends every creature and every act of the knowing power. That peak, I say, *of the mystical Scriptures*: for at that peak (as was said above) God speaks with man and man with God, by that most secret speaking which is not through symbols or images but through unveiled vision. *More than unknown*, because the only one who knows that peak is the one who arrives there (something very few do), and because on it there is the actual privation of all knowledge. *And more than light-filled*, because on it the light which is above every light manifests itself just as, and in so far as, it knows that to be fitting for itself as the giver and suitable for the receiver. *Where*, that is, on that peak, [are] *the mysteries of theology*, that is, the mystical and most secret things of the conversation with God; for in that place mystery and mystic coincide, because what signifies and what is signified

id est secundum divini luminis inaccessibilitatem, que in se est superlucida, et secundum privationem actualis cognitionis et comprehensionis, que est proxima aptitudo ad susceptionem superlucidi luminis; *caliginem silencii occulte docentis*, id est privationis exterius sonantis et multiplicati sermonis ex parte Dei eterno et unico et non exterius perstrepenti verbo occulte docentis, et privationis omnimodi sermonis tam intus disposti quam exterius prolati ex parte existentis in dicto vertice occulte discentis; *superlustrantem*, caliginem videlicet, id est manifestantem *supermanifestissimum*, id est Deum, lumen super omne lumen, *in tenebrosissimo* ipsius videlicet caliginis, et *superimplentem* caliginem, videlicet intellectus iam existentes in dicto vertice, *superpulcris claritatibus* divini videlicet radii superfulgentis et superlustrantis in *omnino intangibili et invisibili*, id est in omnino inaccessibili superiori vel inferiori, virtute ipsius divini radii: in sua enim inaccessibilitate prestat se accessibilem et in sua immensitate moderatur se suscipientis mensure. Huic autem dictioni "intellectus" coniungit auctor in Greco hoc adiectivum *anommatoys*, quod quidam[4] transtulerunt in "invisibiles," et sic est littera latina facilis; sed videtur quod illa dictio greca significet "inoculatos," id est non habentes oculos: *omma* enim est "oculus" et *a* est in greco privativa particula, et sic videtur sensus inconveniens, cum tota essentia intellectus sit spiritalis oculus, et ideo dicuntur intellectus illi supremi "multorum oculorum" et "undique oculati." Sed quia auctor hic intendit de intellectibus humanis qui iam ascenderunt in predictum verticem et in predictam caliginem, in qua otiantur ab omni actu visionis, hoc est omnimode comprehensionis cuiuscumque creati, existimo quod eos vocavit inoculatos non a privatione potentie spiritaliter visive, sed a privatione omnis actus visivi dum otiantur in illa caligine.

Et notandum quod dictio Greca, quam transferunt "in occulto docentis," est una dictio composita a *krifion*, quod est "absconditum," et *myω*, verbo Greco de quo supra diximus; et idem significat tam "occulte docentem" quam "occulte discentem." Sicut enim

---

[4] Eriugena.

is the same, what manifests and what is manifested is the same. *Simple*, because with one simple Word God speaks whatever he speaks, and he is heard by the most simple capacity of the mind. *And absolute*, because without symbol or parable. *And unchanging*, because they have immutable truth. Where, I say, these mysteries *are veiled*, that is, are hidden and covered from the eyes of all those who are living purely as man. *In that brilliant darkness*, that is, relative to the inaccessibility of the divine light, which in itself is more than bright, and relative to the privation of actual knowledge and comprehension, that privation which is the nearest state of preparedness for the reception of the light which is more than bright. *The darkness of the secretly-teaching silence*, that is, the privation of the word that is externally sounding and multiplied, relative to God who is teaching hiddenly with his eternal and unique Word, the Word that does not make noise or clamor exteriorly but teaches hiddenly; and of the privation of any kind of word, whether created within or brought forth without, on the part of the one who is learning hiddenly on that peak. *More than shining* refers to the darkness insofar as it is shining forth. *The one who is beyond showing forth*, that is, God, light above all light. *In the darkest place* and *completely filling* the darkness, that is to say, the intellects which are already on that peak, *with the brightness beyond all beauty*, that is to say, of the divine ray which is more than brightness and more than shining, *in the wholly intangible and invisible*; that is, in the completely inaccessible (whether by higher or by lower power) divine ray itself. For in its own inaccessibility it offers itself as accessible, and in its immensity it limits itself to the measure of the one receiving. To the word *intellectus*, however, the author adds the Greek adjective *anommatous*, which some have translated *invisibilis* — a facile Latin translation, for it appears that the Greek word means *inoculatos*, that is to say, not having any eyes: *omma* is eye, and *a* is the Greek privative particle. Thus the meaning appears contradictory, since the whole essence of intellect is spiritual eye, and for that reason those highest intellects are called "of many eyes" and "with eyes on all sides." But since the author has in mind here human intellects which have already ascended to the mountain peak we have spoken of, and who have gone into the darkness that he has referred to, in which they simply relax from every act of vision (that is, from any kind of comprehension of any sort of creature whatsoever), I consider that he called them eyeless on the basis not of the privation of the power of seeing spiritually but of the privation of every act of sight, for as long as they remain relaxed in that darkness.

It should be noted also that the Greek expression which they translate *in occulto docentis* [teaching in hiddenness] is a composite expression [derived] from *krifion*, "hidden," and *muw*, the Greek verb which we talked of earlier; and it signifies both "someone teaching hiddenly" and "someone learning hiddenly." For just as "darkness" and "silence" in this passage together embrace what is from the divine side and what is from the side of the mind which has attained to the highest peak, so also that Greek word embraces

caligo et silentium in hoc loco comprehendunt communiter quod est ex parte divina et ex parte mentis que attigit ad supremum verticem, sic et illa dictio Greca comprehendit quod est ex parte utraque, quod tamen Latine non exprimitur nisi multipliciori sermone. Postquam autem ipsemet oravit ut sancta Trinitas eum in predictum dirigat supremum verticem, ubi invelata sunt summe mistica in caligine manifestante lumen supermanifestum in tenebrosissimo inaccessibilitatis ipsius et implente intellectus inoculatos superpulcris claritatibus, breviter optat et rogat ut alii orent hoc sibi donari, sic subiungens: *mihi quidem igitur hec orentur.* Perfecta itaque sic oratione, convertit sermonem ad Timotheum, instruens ipsum quibus gradibus et qua sui adaptatione poterit ad dictum verticem pertingere, sic inquiens: *tu autem, o amice Timothee, ea forti attricione,* hoc est ea forti exercitatione, *que circa misticas visiones,* hoc est in forti conatu et labore ad pertingendum ad visiones divinas secretas sine symbolis et ymaginibus, *derelinque et sensus,* hoc est sensuum operationes, *et intellectuales operationes, hoc* est operationes omnes omnium virium apprehensivarum inferiorum et superiorum, *et omnia sensibilia et intelligibilia et omnia non entia et entia,* ut videlicet ad nullum ens vel non ens aliquo affectu inclineris et ei inviscaris et inviscatione cum eo impediaris et retarderis in tuo conatu ad misticas visiones; *et restituere incognite, ut possibile, ad unionem eius qui super omnem substantiam et cognitionem,* que quidem restitutio fit per ipsius solius forte desiderium et amorem superfervidum, que nulli rationativa investigatione potest esse cognita. Et bene te moneo ut in attricione circa misticas visiones hec facias: *ea enim extasi,* id est extrastatione, *irretentibili,* per inviscationem videlicet inordinate affectionis cum aliquo vel ente vel non ente, *et absoluta pure,* id est omnino libera, ea inquam extasi tali *que tui ipsius et omnium,* id est que extra et supra te et omnia reduceris seu sursum *reduceris ad supersubstantialem radium divine tenebre,* id est divine superluciditatis propter suam eminentiam invisibilis; tu, dico *auferens omnia,* a te ipso videlicet, *et absolutus ex omnibus,* hoc est derelinquens omnia, ut predictum est, et nulli inviscatus, vel auferens omnia, ab ipso videlicet divino radio, hoc est per abnegationem omnium ab ipso, accedens ad eius visionem, absolutus, ut predictum est, ex omnibus.

2. Hec autem vide ut nullus indoctorum audiat. Hos autem aio eos qui in existentibus detenti sunt et nihil super entia supersubstantialiter esse ymaginantur, sed existimant scire ea que secundum se ipsos cognitione ponentem tenebram latibulum ipsius [Ps. 17:12]. Si autem super hos sunt divine mistice inductiones, quid utique quis dicat de magis indoctis, quotquot omnibus superpositam causam et ex hiis que in existentibus

what is on both parts, whereas in Latin that can only be expressed by a paraphrase. But after he himself has prayed that the Holy Trinity may guide him to the peak spoken of, where those things which are mystical in the highest degree are veiled in a darkness which both manifests and fills (it manifests the light which is more-than-manifest in the most dark place of its inaccessibility, and it fills those intellects which are deprived of sight with lights which are more than beautiful), in brief words he wishes and asks and prays, that others may pray that this may be given to them, adding, *let these prayers therefore be made by me*. Having finished his prayer thus he turns to Timothy, instructing him by what degrees and by what preparation of himself he will be able to reach the mountain peak he has spoken of, saying: *But you, my friend Timothy, by that strong effort*, that is, by that strong exertion *with regard to the mystical visions*, that is, in the strong straining and effort to reach the secret divine visions without symbols and images, *leave the senses*, that is, the operations of the senses, *and also intellectual operations*, that is, all the operations of all the powers of knowledge both lower and higher, *and all sensibles and intelligibles and all non-beings and beings*, in order that you may not lean towards any being or non-being with affection and be attached to it, and by the attachment to it be impeded and retarded in your straining towards mystical visions. *And return without knowledge, as far as you can, to union with him who is above all being and knowledge*. This return indeed comes about through the strong desire and superfervent love of him alone who cannot be known by anyone through step by step inquiry. And well I warn you to do the following in the exertion regarding the mystical visions: *for by that ecstasy* (that is, by standing outside of oneself) *that cannot be held back* through any disordered attachment to any being or non-being, *and which is purely absolute*, that is, completely free; in such an ecstasy, I say, *of yourself and all things* (that is, things outside, and above you, and above all) *you may be led back* or beyond, *to the supersubstantial ray of divine darkness*, that is, of the divine brightness which is beyond brightness, and which is invisible because of its transcendence. You, I say, *taking away everything* (that means, of course, from yourself) *and cut off from all*, that is, abandoning everything (as has been said), and being attached to nothing, or taking away everything (that is, from the divine ray itself) through denying all things of him: being cut off, as was said, from all things, approach the vision of him.

2. But see that none of the uninformed should hear these things: I mean those people who are retained in existing things and who imagine that there is nothing transcendently beyond the beings, but who think that they know, with the knowledge that is theirs, the One who has made the shadows his hiding place. But if the divine leading into the mysteries is beyond them what indeed is one to say about the even more uninformed,

extremis characterizant et nihil ipsam superexcellere aiunt formatas ab ipsis impias et multiformes formationes?

Quia predicta nec probabilia, nec credibilia sunt indoctis nihil potentibus comprehendere super entia eis cognita, nec ex eorum auditu proficerent sed magis scandalizarentur, iubet auctor Timotheo ut nulli indoctorum ista communicet, quemadmodum in pluribus aliis locis de exsuperantibus multitudinis intelligentiam precepit. Ait igitur: *hec autem vide*, o tu Timothee videlicet, *ut nullus indoctorum audiat*. Quos autem intelligit indoctos, explanat consequenter dicens: *hos autem*, id est indoctos, *aio eos qui in existentibus detenti sunt*, seu informati seu infigurati sunt, *et nihil ymaginantur esse supersubstantialiter super entia, sed existimant scire ponentem tenebram*, id est lucis inaccessibilitatem, *latibulum ipsius, ea cognitione que secundum se ipsos*, id est cognitione tali quali cognoscunt res mundanas et se ipsos. Non est autem, ut liquet ex premissis, tali cognitione Deus cognoscibilis, sed cognitiones inductive in mistica divina videnda plurimum excedunt talium indoctorum cognitiones, et multo magis eorum cognitiones qui confingunt Deo formas corporeas, ut faciunt idolatre. Unde sequitur: *si autem super hos*, predictos videlicet indoctos, quales sunt multi etiam ad fidem conversi, *sunt divine mistice inductiones*, id est inductiones in visionem divinorum secretorum et occultorum, *quid utique dicat quis de magis indoctis quotquot characterizant*, id est formant et figurant *causam superpositam omnibus et*, id est etiam, *ex hiis que in existentibus extremis, et aiunt ipsam nihil superexcellere impias et multiformes formationes formatas ab ipsis?* Faciunt enim ydolatre diis suis varias et impias formationes corporeas, mutantes gloriam incorruptibilis Dei in similitudinem ymaginis corruptibilis hominis et volucrum et quadrupedum et serpentium [Rom 1:23]. "Mistice inductiones" est in Greco una dictio composita et potest exponi etiam in "misticorum" seu "misteriorum inductiones."

3. Opportunum in ipsa et omnes entium ponere et dicere positiones ut omnium causa, et omnes ipsas principalius abnegare ut super omnia superexistente, et non existimare abnegationes oppositas esse affirmationibus,

those who portray the transcendent cause of all things in terms of the lowest of existing things, and who say that it has nothing over and beyond the impious and multiformed shapes composed by themselves?

[Commentary]

Because the foregoing things are neither susceptible of proof nor credible on the part of the uninstructed, who are capable of understanding nothing beyond the beings that are known to them, nor would they draw profit from hearing of those things but rather would be scandalized, the author commands Timothy to communicate those things to none of the uninstructed, just in the same way as in a number of other places he lays down with regard to the transcendent things a restriction regarding the intelligence of the multitude. He says, therefore, *But take care*, Timothy, *that none of the uninstructed should hear these things.* He explains in what follows whom he is referring to as uninstructed, saying, *But those* (that is, the uninstructed) *I speak of are retained in existing things,* or are unformed or unshaped; those *who imagine that there is nothing transcendently beyond the beings, but who think that they know the One who makes the darkness* (that is, the inaccessibility of light) *his hiding place; with the knowledge that is theirs,* that is, by knowledge similar to that by which they know the things of the world and themselves. But God is not knowable (as is quite clear from what has been said) in terms of such knowing. The knowledge which leads to the sight of mystical, divine things far transcends the knowledge of such uninstructed people, and more so still the knowledge of those who make up corporeal forms for God, as idolaters do. Whence he goes on: *But if it is beyond them* (that is to say, the uninstructed ones referred to — even many of those who have converted to the faith are like them), meaning by that *the divine leading into the mysteries* (that is, guidance into the vision of divine, secret and hidden things), *what indeed is one to say about the even more uninformed, who portray* (or, who form and shape) *the transcendent cause of all things in terms even of the lowest of existing things, and who say that it has nothing over and beyond the impious and multiformed shapes composed by themselves?* For idolaters make for their gods various and impious corporeal forms, and change the glory of the incorruptible God into the likeness of the image of a corruptible man, and of birds, and of four-footed beasts, and of creeping things. "Mystical guidance" is a composite word in Greek; it can also be interpreted as "guidance to mystical or mysterious things."

3. We are required to attribute to it all the positive attributes of existent things and to affirm them of it, since it is the cause of all; and more primordially still to deny all of these, since it exists beyond existence, far

sed multum prius ipsam super privationes esse eam que super omnem et ablationem et positionem. Sic igitur divinus Bartholomeus ait et multam theologiam esse et minimam et evangelium latum et magnum et rursus correptum, mihi videtur illud supernaturaliter intelligens quoniam et multorum sermonum est bona omnium causa et brevium sermonum similiter et sine sermone, ut neque sermonem neque intelligentiam habens, propter omnibus ipsam supersubstantialiter superpositam esse et solis incircumvelate et vere manifestam hiis, qui et immunda omnia et pura transcendunt et omnem omnium sanctarum extremitatum ascensionem superascendunt, et omnia divina lumina et sonos et sermones celestes derelinquunt et in caliginem introeunt, ubi vere est, ut eloquia aiunt, qui ultra omnia [Ex. 20:21; cf. Ex. 19:1].

Quoniam proximo redarguit auctor characterizantes Deum ex extremis, et posset ex hoc videri auctorem insinuare ipsum non esse nominabilem et laudabilem ex omnibus positionibus, volens hoc auferre et cum hoc manifestare quod per abnegationes omnium ab ipso directius attingitur ad verticem et caliginem in quibus impletur intellectus superpulcris divini radii claritatibus, adiungit omnium positiones dici de eo, non quia sit aliquod entium, sed quia omnium est causa, et omnium abnegationes, quia ipse est super omnia, quam superioritatem, ut in prioribus sepe pretactum est, insinuant negationes de eo dicte; et quod abnegationes de eo dicte non sunt opposite affirmationibus de ipso dictis, cum ipse sit superius et prius omni abnegatione et sermone et ratione; si enim prius est ipsis, non necessario est alterum in ipso vel de ipso. Hec igitur adiungens ait: *opportunum in ipsa*, id est in superposita omnibus causa, *et omnes entium ponere et dicere positiones ut omnium causa*, id est ut in omnium causa, *et omnes ipsas*, positiones videlicet, *abnegare principalius*, seu magis proprie: vere enim et proprie non est aliquid entium, et non vere et proprie dicitur aliquid entium, *ut superexistente*, id est superexistente *super omnia, et non existimare abnegationes oppositas esse affirmationibus, sed ipsam*, superpositam videlicet omnibus causam, *esse multum prius super privationes*; eternitate enim precedit etiam hoc ipsum non esse, *ipsam*, dico, *eam que super omnem et ablationem et positionem*. In omni creato est suum non esse ante eius esse; in increato autem non sic, sed ipsum precedit omne non esse et simpliciter non esse, et omne esse et simpliciter esse, et ideo non potest circa ipsum immediate compugnare aliqua oppositio.

beyond all things. We are not to suppose that the negations are opposed to the affirmations. Instead we should hold that, being above every removal and every positive attribution, it is prior by far to the privative [use of] terms. And therefore the Bl. Bartholomew says that the Word of God is both vast and tiny, and the Gospel broad and great, and yet concise. He seems to me to have comprehended this supernaturally: that the good cause of things is both of many words and brief ones, and at the same time without a word — meaning by that having neither word nor intelligence, on account of being placed transcendently beyond all things; and it appears unveiled and truly only to those who go beyond things both impure and pure, and who mount above every ascent of all holy and highest realities, and who leave behind all divine lights and sounds and heavenly words and enter into the darkness where, as the Scripture says, he truly is who is above all.

[Commentary]

Because in the immediately foregoing the author has refuted those who characterize God from the lowest things, and because he could appear to be suggesting that God cannot be named and praised on the basis of all positive terms, wishing to remove this misunderstanding, and at the same time to make it clear that the more direct way of access to the peak and the darkness (in which the intellect is filled with the transcendently-beautiful brightness of the divine ray) lies through the negations of all things with regard to him, he adds that the positive sense of all things is said about God, not because God is some one thing among the things that are, but because he is the cause of all things; and the negations of all things likewise, because he is above all things. That superiority, as has often been mentioned in the foregoing, is what is implied by the negations that are expressed concerning him. Also [he adds] that the negations said of God are not opposed to the affirmations made of him, since he is higher and prior to every negation, word, or reason. For if he is something prior to them there is not necessarily any "other" in himself, or with regard to himself. Adding these things, therefore, he says: *To it we are required* (that is, to the cause that is placed beyond all things) *to attribute all the positive attributes of things, since it is the cause of all* (that is, to the cause of all things), *and all of these* (referring to the positive terms) *to deny more primordially* or more properly. For truly and properly speaking he is not some one of the things, and he is not said, truly or properly speaking, to be one of the things, *since he exists beyond existence* (that is, being beyond), *above all things; and [we are required] not to suppose that the negations*

Que autem predicta sunt, licet philosophicis assertionibus videantur dissona, super-naturaliter intellexit beatus Bartholomeus et scripsit, seu forte sine scripto dixit, cuius verba in sui dicti testimonium et confirmationem trahit auctor iste et dicit: *sic igitur divinus Bartholomeus ait et multam esse theologiam*, id est de Deo locutionem esse multam propter omnium positiones et omnium abnegationes de ipso dici, *et minimam* propter ipsum utrisque omnibus preesse et superius esse, et ut est in se et quid est in se nullo modo effabile esse; et propter eadem *evangelium*, id est de Deo annunciationem, *latum et magnum et rursus correptum; mihi videtur intelligens*, Bartholomeus videlicet, per hoc suum dictum *supernaturaliter*, quia super communem hominis naturalem virtutem est ascendere predicto modo in verticem et caliginem ubi talia intelliguntur, intelligens, inquam, *illud quoniam bona omnium causa est et multorum sermonum* seu multiloqua, id est per multas locutiones et multos sermones, quia, ut predictum est, per omnium positiones et ablationes enarrabilis et laudabilis, *et brevium sermonum similiter* seu breviloqua, quia unico verbo positivo, utpote nomine bonitatis, potest comprehendi quicquid de eo positive dicitur, ut patet ex hiis que dicta sunt De Divinis Nominibus, et similiter forte aliquo uno nomine privativo potest comprehendi omne dictum de eo privative; et insuper quoniam est *sine sermone ut neque habens sermonem*, qui videlicet eum enarret ut est et quid est in se, *neque intelligentiam*, que videlicet ut est et quid est in se eum intelligat; *propter ipsam*, primam videlicet causam, *esse superpositam supersubstantialiter omnibus et manifestam incircumvelate et vere*, id est absque symbolis et ymaginibus secundum sui nudam superapparitionem *solis hiis qui transcendunt immunda omnia*, id est hec terrena, que, amore contacta, maculant amantem, *et pura* que, mente contacta, non maculant contingentem, *et superascendunt ascensionem*, id est ascendunt super ascensionem, *omnium sanctarum extremitatum*, seu summitatum, id est virium apprehensivarum secundum extremum et summum sue possibilitatis agentium, quod non faciunt nisi sancte, hoc est ascendunt super summos actus omnis virtutis apprehensive agentis, quantum possibile est, intense; *et derelinquunt omnia divina lumina*, illustrantia videlicet vires apprehensivas, ut agant proprias actiones in quantum sic illustrantia, *et sonos et sermones celestes*, id est actuales instructiones spiritales angelicas vel ex sacra scriptura susceptibiles, *et introeunt in caliginem*, id est actualem ignorantiam omnium, *ubi vere est, ut eloquia aiunt, qui ultra omnia*; solum enim ibi vere invenitur et tenetur, et qualis ibi invenitur non est effabilis homini, et propter hoc bene dicitur "sine sermone."

are opposed to the affirmations, but that it (that is, the cause of all things that is placed above all) *is by far prior to the privative* [use of] *terms.* For by eternity he precedes even this same non-being, *being* (I say) *above both every removal and every positive attribution.* In every created being its non-being is before its being; but in the uncreated it is not so, rather he precedes every non-being, and non-being simply, and every being, and being simply. Therefore no contradiction can fight with itself immediately about him.

What has been said, however, even though it seems out of harmony with philosophical assertions, is what the Bl. Bartholomew understood supernaturally and wrote down (or perhaps said, without writing it): those words this author draws upon in testimony and confirmation of his own statement, and says, *So, therefore, the Bl. Bartholomew says the Word of God is both vast* (that is, speech concerning God is great, for the reason that the affirmations of all things and the negations of all things are said of God), *and tiny,* because of his pre-existing and being superior to all statements of both kinds, and he is in no way sayable as he is in himself and what he is in himself. For the same reasons *the Gospel* (that is, what is announced concerning God) *is broad and great and yet concise. He appears to be understanding* (he is referring through this statement to Bartholomew) *supernaturally,* because it is above the common, natural power of man to ascend in the way that has been said to the summit and the darkness, where such things are understood; understanding, as I said, *that the good cause of things is both of many words* (or many-speaking, that is, through many statements and many words, because as was said already, God can be spoken of and praised through the affirmations of all things and through their negations); *and also brief ones,* or summary words, because whatever can be said concerning him positively can be comprehended in one single, positive word, which is to say the name of the good, as is clear from what has been said concerning the *Divine Names*; and similarly perhaps by any one privative name everything that is said concerning him privatively can be understood. And moreover, since he is *without a word as not having a word* (one, that is to say, which speaks him as he is, and says what he is in himself), *nor intelligence,* which understands him as he is and what he is in himself; *on account of its* (meaning, the first cause) *being placed transcendently beyond all things and appearing unveiled and truly,* that is, without symbols and images, in its naked apparition, *only to those who go beyond all impure things,* that is, these earthly things, which when touched with love soil the lover, *and pure* which, touched by the mind, do not soil the one touching, *and mount above every ascent* (that is, they ascend beyond the ascent) *of all holy and highest realities,* or heights, that is, of the powers of knowledge acting according to the extreme and highest of their capacities; which they do not do unless these powers of the mind are holy. That is, they ascend above the highest acts of every power of knowledge in act, stretched out as far as is possible; *and who leave behind all divine lights* (that is to say, lighting up the powers of apprehension, that they may do their own actions by being illumined) *and sounds and heavenly words,*

Que autem diximus "multorum sermonum" seu "multiloqua," et "brevium sermonum" seu "breviloqua," et "sine sermone," quod si latine diceretur, posset dici "inloqua," sunt in Greco singule dictiones composite; et quod in illis compositionibus ponitur in insinuationem locutionis seu sermonis posset intelligi active, sicut in hac dictione
"multiloquum," sed menti auctoris et sensui littere circumstantis, ut existimo, non con-
sonaret.

4. Etenim non simpliciter divinus Moyses repurgare primum ipsum iussus est et rursus a non talibus segregari, et post omnem repurgationem
audit multivocas tubas et videt lumina multa puros fulgurantia et multipliciter fusos radios [cf. Ex. 19:20; 20:18–21]; deinde a multis segregatur
et cum electis sacerdotibus ad summitatem divinarum ascensionum pertingit et in hiis ipsi quidem non confit deo, contemplatur autem non
ipsum, invisibilis enim, sed locum ubi stetit. Hoc autem existimo significare divinissima et summa visorum et intellectorum ypoteticos quosdam
esse sermones suppositorum omnia superexcedenti, per que ea que super
omnem cogitationem ipsius presentia ostenditur intelligibilibus summitatibus sanctissimorum ipsius locorum superascendens, et tunc et ab ipsis
absolvitur visis et videntibus et in caliginem ignorantie intrat vere misticam, secundum quam excludit easdem cognoscitivas susceptiones, et in
omnino impalpabili et invisibili fit omnium eius qui ultra omnia et nullius neque sui ipsius neque alterius perfecte autem incogniti omnis cognitionis inoperationem secundum melius unitus, et nihil cognoscere super
intellectum cognoscens.

Ordinem predictum ascensionis in caliginem, ubi vere est Deus qui ultra omnia, et in
qua vere et incircumvelate manifestatur, significavit quod in Moyse factum est, unde et
in testimonium predictorum inducit auctor enarrationem circa Moysen factorum, dicens:

that is, the actual angelic, spiritual instructions, or those that can be received from holy Scripture, *and enter into the darkness*, that is, into the actual unknowing of all things, *where he truly is, as the Scriptures say, who is above all*; for only there is he truly found and truly held; and as he is found there he is not sayable to any man, and for that reason he is well said to be "without a word."

But the words that we have rendered *multiloqua* [of many words], and *breviloqua* [of short words] and "without word" (which, if it were said in Latin would be *inloqua*) are in each case composite words in Greek. What is placed in those composites in order to suggest speech or word could be understood actively, as in the word *multiloquum* ["much-speaking"]; but such would not agree, I feel, with the mind of the author and with the sense of the ambient text.

4. Yet it was not purely for its own sake that the Bl. Moses was commanded first to purify himself and then to be separated from those who are not pure. And after the whole purification he hears the many-voiced trumpets; he sees the many lights flashing pure and abundantly-streaming rays. Afterwards he is segregated from the crowd and reaches the summit of the divine ascents with the chosen priests, even though he is not by that fact with God, but he contemplates, not him — for he is invisible — but the place where he is. I take it, however, that this signifies that the most divine and highest of the things seen and understood are certain hypothetical words of things subject to the One who transcends all. Through them his presence, which is above all thought, is shown going up on high to the intelligible summits of his most holy places. And then [Moses] is set free from what is seen and those that see, and enters into the truly mystical darkness of unknowing. In this state he closes off all that the mind may receive and enters into the altogether intangible and invisible, belonging completely to him who is beyond everything, and belonging to no [other], neither himself nor anyone else. And through complete liberation from all knowledge, united in his better part to the perfectly Unknown, he is knowing beyond the mind — by knowing nothing.

[Commentary]

What was done in Moses referred to the aforementioned order of the ascent into the darkness, where God truly is who is beyond all things, and in which he is manifested truly and without any veil around him. And so in testimony of the aforementioned

etenim non simpliciter, id est non propter solum nudum actum exteriorem, sed magis propter significatum spiritale[5] *divinus Moyses iussus est repurgare primum ipsum*, id est se ipsum, *et rursus segregari a non talibus*, id est a non puris et non purgatis, *et post omnem repurgationem audit multivocas* seu multisonas *tubas et videt lumina multa fulgurantia* seu choruscantia, id est ad modum fulguris choruscantis emittentia *puros radios et multipliciter fusos*, seu si latine diceretur unica dictione, "multifusos," *deinde a multis*, id est a populi multitudine *segregatur, et cum electis sacerdotibus pertingit ad summitatem divinarum ascensionum*, id est graduum ascensionis in montem, *et in hiis*, id est in predictis omnibus *non confit*, seu non coest, *ipsi quidem Deo*, ut videlicet ipsum adhuc videat et loquatur cum ipso sicut fecit in caligine; *contemplatur autem non ipsum*, id est Deum, *invisibilis enim, sed locum ubi stetit*, id est locum caliginis, *et tunc absolvitur* ipse Moyses *et ab ipsis visis*, id est exterioribus visibilibus, *et videntibus*, populis videlicet et sacerdotibus qui cum eo ascenderant: non enim ulterius ea vice vidit hec exteriora visibilia, vel qui cum eo ascenderant viderunt ipsum et in caliginem intrare.

Hoc modo est ordinanda compositio littere ad nudam explanationem hystorie. Interponit autem misticam significationem eius quod est ipsum videre locum ubi stetit Deus, et adiungit misticam significationem caliginis, et quod spiritaliter fit in mistica caligine spiritaliter significata per reliqua historica que hic narrantur, utpote intellectu facilia, relinquens lectoris diligentie. Satis enim liquidum est quod Moysi purgatio historica significat spiritalem purgationem ab omni inordinato appetitu qui solus maculat, segregatio vero a non purgatis significat quod in nullo immundo eis consentit, sed omnem immundorum immunditiam detestatur. Post hanc spiritalem purgationem fit homo interior aptus ad audiendam et intelligendam scripturam, cuius tube multivoce sunt symbolice dicta multipliciter multa significantia; lumina vero multa sunt spiritalia significata per symbola a materialibus sumpta, que puros et multimode fusos radios mittunt in humanas intelligentias clarificandas. In hiis autem communicant multi: intellectum enim scripture hystoricum et allegoricum et moralem habent multi, sed interior homo, querens videre Deum incircumvelate et vere, hiis non est contentus, sed ab hiis se segregans et hos transcendens, ascendit cum electis et sacris contemplativis et doctoribus ad summitatem anagogicorum intellectuum, in quibus tamen omnibus non confit ipsi Deo ut videat ipsum nude sine symbolis et ymaginibus, sed in hiis solum contemplatur locum ubi stetit Deus. In anagogia enim nondum videtur Deus nude et

---

[5] spiritale] spiritalem MSS

things the author brings in an account of the things done concerning Moses, saying: *yet it is not purely for its own sake*, that is, not on account of the mere naked, external act, but rather on account of the thing signified *that the Bl. Moses was commanded first to purify him*, that is, himself, *and then to be separated from those that are not such*, that is, from those who are not pure or purified. *And after the whole purification he hears the many-voiced* (or the many-sounding) *trumpets and he sees the many lights flashing* (or coruscating, that is, emitting rays like lightning flashing) *pure and abundantly-streaming rays*, or if it were to be said in Latin in one word, *multifusos* ["many-streaming"]. *Afterwards from the crowd* (that is, from the multitude of the people) *he is segregated, and with the chosen priests he reaches the summit of the divine ascents*, that is, of the steps of the ascent up the mountain, *and in them* (that is, in all the aforementioned things) *he does not come to be with* (or he is not with) *God himself*, to be able to see him still and speak with him as he did in the darkness. *But he contemplates not him*, that is God (*for he is invisible*), *but the place where he stood* (that is, the place of the darkness). *And then* [Moses himself] *is set free both from what is seen* (that is, exterior, visible things) *and from those that see* (the people, that is, and the priests who had gone up with him; for on that occasion he did not any longer see these exterior, visible things, nor did those who had gone up with him see him as he was going into the darkness.

This is the way in which the composition of the literal sense is ordered for the unadorned explanation of the story. But he interjects a mystical meaning of seeing "the place where God stood," and he adds the mystical signification of the darkness and what is done spiritually in the mystical darkness, spiritually signified by the remaining historical features which are narrated here, leaving these to the diligence of the reader as being easy to understand. It is fairly evident that the historical purgation of Moses signifies spiritual purgation from every inordinate appetite, which alone soils one. But the segregation from the unpurified signifies that he consents with them in nothing that is unclean, but detests every uncleanness of the unclean. After this spiritual purification the interior man becomes able to hear and understand the Scriptures, whose many-voiced trumpets are spoken of symbolically in several ways which have multiple significance. The many-signifying lights, on the other hand, are signified spiritually by means of symbols taken from material things, which send pure and variously-streaming rays in order to illuminate human intelligences. In these, however, the many communicate, for the crowd have the understanding of Scripture that is historical and allegorical and moral, but the interior man, seeking to see God without veil and truly, is not content with these things, but separating himself off from the many and moving beyond them, he ascends with the elect and the sacred contemplatives and teachers to the summit of the anagogic understandings. In all of these, however, he is not placed before God himself in order that he may see him nakedly, without symbols and images, but in these he contemplates only "the place where God stood." For in anagogy God is not yet seen

incircumvelate, sed in ea speculamur ipsum in omnibus creaturis quasi in quibusdam vestigiis ipsius, et in creaturis inferioribus quasi in quibusdam vestigiis minus formatis, et in creaturis superioribus quasi in vestigiis formatioribus, et in summis quasi in formatissimis. Et propter hoc in anagogia videtur solum locus ubi Deus stetit, inquantum est locus sue stationis, et summa et divinissima visa et intellecta inquantum talia, id est in quantum eius loca sunt quidam interiores mentis sermones non prolocutivi ipsius Dei in se, sed suppositorum ipsi, inquantum per ea manifestatur eius presentia nuda in se superexcedens omnem summitatem omnis et summe et sanctissime creature.

Et hoc est quod interponendo ait auctor: *hoc autem*, quod videlicet contemplatur non ipsum Deum sed locum ubi stetit, *existimo significare* hoc scilicet *divinissima et summa visorum et intellectorum*, anagogice videlicet, *esse quosdam sermones ypoteticos*, id est suppositivos, hoc est non excelsissimos significantes nude Deum, sed suppositivos, significativos videlicet *suppositorum superexcedenti omnia, per que*, id est inquantum per ea, *ostenditur ea presentia* videlicet *super omnem cogitationem, superascendens intelligibilibus summitatibus sanctissimorum locorum ipsius*, id est sanctissimaram creaturarum retinentium eius vestigia tanquam loca in quibus stetit. *Et tunc*, id est postquam ascendit cum electis doctoribus ad summitatem anagogicorum intellectuum, cum iam relinquitur creatura in qua ulterius possit queri desideratus, *absolvitur et ab ipsis visis*, id est ab omnibus sensibilibus et intelligibilibus ea derelinquens, *et videntibus*, id est sensitivis et intellectualibus operationibus, *et intrat in caliginem ignorantie*; absolutus enim a visis et videntibus, id est ab apprehensibilibus et operationibus apprehensivis, necessario consequenter fit in caligine actualis ignorantie omnium et intrat eam *vere misticam*, quia secretissime secretissimi edoctivam et disciplinativam, in ea enim ostendet se divinus radius vere et incircumvelate; et iterum vere misticam quia obscuram, constrictam et clausam; *secundum quam*, caliginem videlicet, *excludit easdem susceptiones cognoscitivas*, hoc est de eisdem, de quibus pretactum est per hoc nomen "videntibus," operationes cognoscitivas que, ut directe agant, indigent susceptione illuminationis dirigentis. In hac enim caligine non solum otiatur quantum ex parte sui ab actibus apprehensivis, sed nec suscipit influentias motivas in actus apprehensivos, et ita est in perfecta actuali ignorantia omnium creatorum et insuper in ignorantia omnium divinorum, unde subiungit: *et fit in omnino impalpabili et invisibili*, id est in omnino incognoscibili, *omnium eius qui ultra omnia*, id est omnium que Dei sunt, et fit, resume, *nullius unitus*, id est nulli creature unitus, *neque sui ipsius neque alterius*; neque enim sibi ipsi neque alteri creature unitur in illa caligine per desiderium aut amorem ipsius *perfecte autem incogniti*, hoc est secundum perfecte incogniti *inoperationem*, id est secundum inoperationem omnis cognitionis fit unitus *secundum melius*, id est secundum supremum virtutis desiderative et amative. Et est Greco more convenientur dictum: "unitus inoperationem": cessans

nakedly and without veil, but in it we contemplate him in all creatures, as though in certain vestiges of himself: in the inferior creatures as though in inferior, less-formed vestiges, and in higher creatures as in more-formed vestiges, and in the highest creatures as in the most-formed. And for this reason, in anagogy only "the place where God stood" is seen, in so far as it is the place of his standing, and the highest and the most divine things seen and understood in so far as they are such, that is, in so far as his "places" are certain interior words of the mind which are not expressive of God himself in himself, but which stand in the place of him, in so far as through them his naked presence in himself, far transcending every summit of every highest and most holy creature, is manifested.

And this is what the author interposes: *But this* (meaning, that which contemplates not God himself, but "the place where he stood") *I take it, signifies* this: *that the most divine and the highest of the things seen and contemplated*, anagogically, he means, *are certain hypothetical words*, that is, lower-placed, not the most exalted [words] nakedly signifying God but lower-placed ones, that is to say, referring *to things subject to the One who transcends all; through which*, that is, in so far as through them, *his presence is shown* which is *above all thought, going up on high to the intelligible summits of his most holy places*, that is, of the most holy creatures which retain vestiges of him, as places in which he has stood. *And then*, that is, after he has ascended with the chosen doctors to the very height of the anagogic understandings, when already the creature is abandoned in which the one desired might be sought further, [Moses] *is set free both from what is seen*, that is, from all sensibles and intelligibles, leaving them behind, *and from those seeing*, that is, sensitive and intellectual operations, *and enters the darkness of unknowing*. For, having been cut off from things seen and from those seeing, that is from things that can be known and from the powers of knowing, he is necessarily placed following that in the darkness of the actual unknowing of all things and enters that truly mystical [darkness, called so] because it both teaches and learns secretly about the most secret one. For in it the divine ray will show itself truly and without any veil; and it is truly mystical in another sense, because it is dark, confined and closed. *In it* (the darkness, he means) *he closes off what the mind may receive*, that is, relative to those things about which we spoke above under the word "seeing": the operations of knowledge which, in order to act directly, require the reception of illumination guiding them. For in this darkness he not only rests as regards all acts of knowing, he does not receive any influences moving him towards acts of knowing. And so he is in complete actual unknowing of all created things; in unknowing, moreover, of all divine things. That is why he adds: *and is in the altogether intangible and invisible*, that is in the wholly unknowable, *of all those things of the One who is beyond everything*, that is, of all those things which are of God. And he comes to be, in short, *united to none*, that is, united to no creature, *neither himself nor anyone else*; for he is united neither to his very own self, nor to another creature in that

enim in illa caligine ab operatione omnis cognitionis secundum estuans desiderium solius Dei perfecte ab ipso incogniti; *et cognoscens,* in illa videlicet caligine, *super intellectum,* quia ad hoc cognoscendum non posset intellectus attingere, cognoscens, inquam, super intellectum *nihil cognoscere,* hoc est se nihil cognoscere.

Hii sunt igitur gradus ascensionis in spiritalem caliginem significati per facta historice a Moyse et circa Moysen, et is est modus habendi se in illa caligine donec radius divinus vere et incircumvelate superappareat dicto modo in caligine expectanti, et ei se revelet ut novit decens et dignum. Et hec huius radii illustratio et illustrationis susceptio mistica est theologia, quia secretissima Dei et cum Deo locutio et sermocinatio. Ordo autem historie factorum a Moyse secundum presentem narrationem evidentior est, ut existimo, ex translatione Septuaginta, quam ex ea qua utitur nostra ecclesia. Per hoc autem quod adiungit hoc nomen "ignorantie" ad hoc nomen "caliginem," ostendit illam historialem caliginem, et per hoc cetera historialiter dicta spiritaliter intelligenda. Quod autem nos diximus "excludit," diversi diversimode transtulerunt.[6] Verbum enim Grecum ibi positum est *apomyei,* compositum ab *apo* prepositione et *myo* verbo cuius significationes supra diximus. Quidam igitur reputantes compositum et simplex idem significare transtulerunt illud secundum aliquam dictarum significationum, alii vero, existimantes prepositionem in compositione immutare significationem simplicis, aliter transtulerunt, unusquisque, prout credidit sensui quem concepit aptius convenire.

CAPITULUM SECUNDUM

QUALITER OPORTET ET UNIRI ET YMNOS REPONERE OMNIUM CAUSE ET SUPER OMNIA

1. Secundum hanc nos fieri superlucidam oramus caliginem, et per invisibilitatem et ignorantiam videre et cognoscere, quod super visionem et

---

[6] Eriugena: *per quam docet*; Sarrazen: *in qua claudit*; Hilduin: *perdiscat.* The confusion between two different verbs gave rise to this diversity: μυέω ("to initiate, to instruct"), and μύω ("to close").

darkness by desire or love of it. *But to the completely unknown*, that is, in so far as it is perfectly unknown, through *non-operation*, that is to say, according to the non-operation of all cognition, he comes to be united *in his better part*, that is, according to the highest part of the power of desiring and loving. And one can say quite acceptably in Greek idiom *unitus inoperationem*; for yielding up in that darkness all cognitive operation, with burning desire of God alone, who is perfectly unknown by him; *and knowing*, he means in that darkness, *beyond the mind*, because the mind could not arrive at the knowledge of that; knowing, I say, beyond the mind, *knows nothing*, that is, that one knows nothing.

These, therefore, are the steps of the ascent to the spiritual darkness. They are signified through the things done historically by Moses and in his regard. And this is the way of behaving in that darkness, until the divine ray may appear mysteriously, truly and without a veil, to the one who is waiting in the darkness, as has been described, and may reveal itself to him as it knows him to be fitting and worthy. And the illumination of this ray and the reception of the illumination is mystical theology, because it is the most secret speaking and talking of God and with God. However, the order of the story of the things done by Moses according to the present account is more evident, I think, from the Septuagint version that from the one which our Church uses. But by the fact that he adds the word "unknowing" to "darkness" he shows that the historical darkness, and thereby also other things that are recounted historically, is to be understood spiritually. Where we have put "he closes off," different translations have been proposed. The Greek word at that point is *apomyei*, composed of *apo* (preposition) and *myω* (verb; meaning discussed above.) But some, taking the complex and the simple to signify the same, translated this according to some of the meanings mentioned, while others, thinking that the preposition in the composite alters the meaning of the single word, translated otherwise — each one just as he believed was better suited to bring out the sense he understood.

CHAPTER II

[Title] HOW IT IS NECESSARY TO BE UNITED TO THE CAUSE OF ALL AND TO GIVE BACK PRAISE

1. We pray to come to this darkness beyond brightness, and by not seeing and not knowing to see and know that this not-seeing and not-knowing is beyond seeing and knowing. For this is truly to see and to know, and to praise the transcendent One in a transcendent way through the

cognitionem hoc non videre neque cognoscere. Hoc enim est vere videre et cognoscere et supersubstantialem supersubstantialiter laudare per omnium entium ablationem, quemadmodum per se naturale agalma facientes, auferentes omnes superadiectas pure occulti visioni prohibitiones, et ipsam in seipsa ablatione sola occultam manifestantes pulcritudinem.

Manifestato per quos gradus ascensionis pervenitur in caliginem, ubi vere est Deus, que caligo est in transcensu mentis super omnia actualis omnium ignorantia superfervido amore videndi eum vere et incircumvelate qui est super omnia, absorbente omnes actus omnium virium apprehensivarum et cognoscitivarum, et inaccessibilitas divini luminis; hec enim duo, ut pretactum est, integrant illam caliginem, licet utraque per se alicubi dicatur caligo; hoc, inquam, manifestato orat auctor se fieri secundum hanc caliginem et se videre per invisibilitatem, que est ex parte inaccessibilitatis divini luminis, et per ignorantiam ex parte videntis, hoc, scilicet quoniam non contingit videre vel cognoscere quod super visionem et cognitionem, id est divinam naturam. Hoc enim est vere videre secundum quod ibi esse potest videre, quemadmodum si homo, superelevans visum suum corporeum super omnia corporaliter visibilia et ocians ab actuali visione omnium, intendens visum suum in solem absque medio mitigante et modificante superexcellentiam solaris claritatis, per invisibilitatem ex parte superexcellentie solaris luminis et privationem actualis visionis videret quoniam non contingit videre solem qui est super visionem: hoc esset ei vere videre secundum quod ibi posset esse videre. In videndo autem per invisibilitatem et ignorantiam quoniam non videtur divina natura, quod est vere videre ipsam secundum quod possibile, videtur etiam quoniam nihil est entium, et aufert mens ab ipsa omnia, et eius pulcritudinem, ut possibile est, per omnium ablationem ab ea sibi denudat et manifestat, et hoc est eam supersubstantialiter laudare in illa caligine. Per superfervidum itaque amorem absorbentem omnes alios actus et in solum Deum tendentem, unitur mens Deo in hac caligine, et per omnium ab eo ablationem absque sermone prolativo eum laudat. Is igitur est modus quo oportet in illa caligine uniri et ymnos reponere omnium cause que est super omnia, et que etiam unio et que ymnorum repositio est super omnia. Orans itaque auctor hec predicta, ait: *secundum hanc nos fieri superlucidam oramus caliginem*, hoc est oramus nos fieri dignos et aptos esse in hac caligine, et dignificatos et aptatos esse in ea, que ex parte inaccessibilitatis divini luminis est superlucida, et ex parte ignorantie in transcensu mentis super omnia est preparatio ad susceptionem divini luminis incircumvelate, ut pretactum est; *et* oramus, resume, *per invisibilitatem*, que videlicet est ex parte superexcellentie divini luminis, *et ignorantiam*, que videlicet est ex parte ascendentis, *videre et cognoscere hoc* scilicet *non videre neque cognoscere quod super visionem et cognitionem*, id est divinam

taking away of all existing things — just as those who make a statue from
life take away the encumbrances to the pure sight of what is hidden, and
by the simple act of taking away they bring to light the hidden beauty.

[Commentary]

Having brought out the steps of ascent by which to get into the darkness where God
truly is, the darkness which is the actual unknowing of all things in the passing upwards
of the mind above all, by the very fervent love of seeing him truly and without veil who
is above all things: that love absorbs all the acts of all the apprehending and knowing
powers. [The darkness is also] the inaccessibility of the divine light. These two factors
(as has already been said) together make up that darkness, even though either taken by
itself is at some point called darkness. Having shown all this, the author prays that he
may be related to this darkness and that by means of the invisibility which comes from
the inaccessibility of the divine light, and through unknowing on the part of the seer,
he may see this: (that is) that one cannot see or know what is above sight and knowledge, that is, the divine nature. For this is truly to see (in so far as is possible to see there):
take the example of a man who raised up his corporeal power of vision above all things
that are corporeally visible, and rested from the actual vision of all things and directed
his vision to the sun, without any medium which might at once mitigate and moder-
ate the transcendent excellence of the solar brightness; through invisibility on the part
of the transcendent excellence of the solar light and the privation of actual vision, he
would see that it is not possible to see the sun, which is above vision: that is what truly
seeing would be for him — in the measure that seeing could take place there at all. However, in seeing through invisibility and unknowing that the divine nature is not seen (and
this is truly to see it — insofar as that is possible), one also sees that it is nothing of the
beings, and the mind then takes away from it all things and it lays bare and manifests
its beauty, insofar as that is possible, through the taking away of all things from it. Now
this precisely is to praise it, [and to do so] in that darkness in a manner beyond being.
And so through the very fervent love's absorbing all the other acts and tending towards
God alone, the mind is united to God in this darkness, and through the removal of all
things from him it praises him without a word of expression. This, therefore, is the
degree to which it is necessary to be united in that darkness, and to render praise to the
cause of all things which is above all things. And this union and this returning of praise
is above all things. And so, praying for these things the author says: *We pray to come to
this darkness beyond brightness*, that is, we pray that we may be made worthy and fitting
to be in this darkness, and we pray to have been made worthy and made apt to be in

naturam in sua superexcellentia; hoc *enim,*[7] id est per invisibilitatem et ignorantiam videre istud *non videre neque cognoscere* divinam naturam, id est quoniam non contingit videre neque cognoscere divinam naturam, *est vere videre et cognoscere*; verius enim et perspicacius non videtur quam cum videtur eius invisibilitas et incognoscibilitas.

Secundum hunc itaque modum ordinandi litteram hec dictio *hoc* prius posita immediate suscipit appositionem huius *non videre neque cognoscere*, et istud est simul iunctum *hoc non videre neque cognoscere*; accusativus sequens istud *per invisibilitatem et ignorantiam videre et cognoscere* et istud *quod super visionem et cognitionem*, est accusativus sequens istud *hoc non videre neque cognoscere*. Potest autem, eodem sensu manente, istud *non videre neque cognoscere* esse accusativus ut prius, quod patet per articulum ei prepositum, et hec dictio *hoc* prius positum sequi accusative ad *non videre neque cognoscere*, et sic ordinari littera: *et per invisibilitatem et ignorantiam videre et cognoscere non videre neque cognoscere hoc quod super visionem et cognitionem.* In primo autem aspectu littere videtur hec particula *quod super visionem et cognitionem* immediate sequi in ordine constructionis ad *videre et cognoscere*, sed si sic ordinaretur constructio hec particula *non videre neque cognoscere*, que ponitur ibi causaliter propter articulum ei prepositum, careret ordine constructionis nec conveniret menti auctoris.

Et oramus, resume, *laudare supersubstantialem*, Deum videlicet, *supersubstantialiter*, id est insinuando eius superexcellentiam super omnem substantiam et essentiam, *per omnium entium ablationem quemadmodum facientes agalma*, id est ymaginem per incisionem, *per se naturale*, id est quod natura totaliter peregit ante artificis operationem, *auferentes*, per incisionem videlicet, omnes *superadiectas prohibitiones*, seu si latine diceretur, "omnia superadiecta prohibimenta," *pure visioni occulti*, id est agalmatis occultati sub prohibentibus puram visionem attingere ad ipsum, *et manifestantes ablatione sola*, superadiectarum videlicet partium materie agalmatis prohibentium et obstantium visioni, *ipsam pulcritudinem in seipsa occultam.* Statuifex itaque, cum ex lapide vel ligno incidendo facit statuam, nihil ei imprimit vel adicit, sed solum auferendo partes materie exteriores

---

[7] See following paragraph.

it. From the side of the inaccessibility of the divine light it [the darkness] is filled with brightness, and from the side of the unknowing in the passing upwards of the mind above all things, there is preparation for the reception of the divine light without any veil around it. And (as was said already) we pray, that is, *through invisibility* (which is, of course, from the side of the divine light's transcendence) *and unknowing* (which is from the side of the one mounting up), *to see and to know this* (meaning): *not to see and not to know what [is] beyond seeing and knowing*, that is, the divine nature in its super-excellence. *For this* (that is, to see it through invisibility and unknowing) *not seeing and not knowing* the divine nature (that is, because it does not in fact see or know the divine nature) *is truly to see and to know*: for it is not seen in any truer or more limpid way than when its invisibility and unknowability is seen.

According to this way of ordering the text the word *this* (used above) immediately receives in apposition the phrase, *not seeing and not knowing*, and this follows immediately upon *this not seeing and not knowing*, the accusative following: *through invisibility and unknowing to see and to know;* and the phrase *what is above vision and knowledge* is the accusative following: *this not seeing and not knowing*. On the other hand that accusative, *not seeing and not knowing*, can be the accusative as before, without the sense being changed. This is clear from the article preceding it and the word *this* before it; it follows in the accusative upon *not to see and not to know*, and in that case the word order would be as follows: *And through invisibility and unknowing to see and to know the not-seeing and not-knowing [of] that which is above vision and knowledge.* At first sight, however, the phrase *what [is] above vision and knowledge* appears to follow immediately in the order of construction upon *to see and to know*; but if the construction were to be taken in that way then the phrase *not seeing and not knowing*, which is placed there in a causal sense given by the article preceding it, would lack order in the construction, and would not agree with the mind of the author.

Back to "We pray": *To praise the transcendent One* (God, of course) *in a transcendent way*, that is, by implying his transcendence of all substance and essence, *through the taking away of all existing things; just as those who are making a statue*, that is, an image, by cutting *something natural in itself*, that is, what nature has completely prepared before the work of the artist, *remove* by incision *all the added encumbrances*, or, if that could be said in Latin, *omnia superadiecta prohibimenta*, which have been added on *to the pure sight of what is hidden*, that is, to attain to the pure vision of the statue hidden under these encumbrances, *and bring to light by the simple act of taking away* the parts added to the matter of the statue and which are prohibitive (or obstructive) of vision, *the hidden beauty*. And so a statue maker, when he makes a statue from stone or wood through chipping away, does not impress anything upon it or add anything to it, but simply by taking away the exterior parts of the matter which obstruct our vision from seeing what is hidden under them, he uncovers and shows forth the shape, color and beauty, and other

que prohibebant visum a visione occultati sub ipsis, detegit et manifestat figuram, colorem et pulcritudinem et cetera sensibilia que natura prius operatione naturali in esse adduxerat. Sic et exsistens in illa caligine omnia ad eum, qui super omnia, visum pertingere nude et incircumvelate prohibentia ab eo auferens, ablatione sola non discursiva per omnia et actu apprehensiva ablatorum, sicut fit extra caliginem, sed per invisibilitatem et ignorantiam perceptiva, quoniam qui super omnia nihil est omnium, denudat et manifestat eius occultam pulcritudinem.

2. Oportet autem, ut existimo, ablationes contrarie positionibus laudare. Etenim illas quidem a prestantissimis inchoantes et per media ad ultima descendentes ponebamus, hic autem ab ultimis ad principalissima ascensiones facientes omnia auferimus, ut incircumvelate cognoscamus illam ignorantiam ab omnibus cognitis in omnibus existentibus velatam, et supersubstantialem illam videamus caliginem ab omni eo, quod in existentibus, lumine occultatam.

In dicta caligine laudatur Deus per omnium ablationem modo quo predictum est, non autem per positiones, quia tunc non esset in ea actualis omnium ignorantia. Extra caliginem vero laudatur per utrasque et principalius per ablationes, et familiarius perducit laus eius per abnegationes ad caliginem et ignorantiam que est in caligine, quod volens auctor declarare, assignat contrarium incessum laudis per ablationes ad eam que per positiones, dicens: *Oportet autem, ut existimo, laudare ablationes contrarie positionibus*, hoc est in laudando Deum per ablationes, contraria via incedere ei qua inceditur in laude eius per positiones. *Etenim illas quidem*, id est positiones, *ponebamus*, seu posuimus, ut oportuit, videlicet *inchoantes a prestantissimis et descendentes per media ad ultima*. In Theologicis enim Subfigurationibus laudavit positive Deum secundum quod ipse est unus et trinus, in libro autem De Divinis Nominibus laudavit ipsum per intelligibiles Dei nominationes, in Symbolica vero Theologia a sensibilibus symbolicis Dei nominationibus, sic a prestantissimis descendens per media ad ultima. *Hic autem*, id est in ascensu ad verticem misticorum eloquiorum, *facientes ascensiones ab ultimis*, id est a sensibilibus, *ad principalissma, auferimus omnia ut incircumvelate cognoscamus illam ignorantiam*, id est divini luminis inaccessibilitatem incognoscibilem, *velatam ab omnibus cognitis in omnibus exsistentibus*; quicquid enim est cognitum in quocumque existente, velamen est ipsius superexcellentie, *et videamus illam supersubstantialem caliginem*, hoc est eandem luminis inaccessibilitatem, *occultatam*, ipsa videlicet sui inaccessibilitate, *ab omni eo*

sensible qualities which nature had already brought into being by its natural operation. Similarly, the one who is in that darkness, taking away from him all that impedes him from attaining nakedly and without veil to the sight of him who is above all things, by a single removal, one that does not run through all things and apprehend in act all the things negated (as is done outside of the darkness), but which knows through invisibility and unknowing that the One who is above all is nothing of all, strips and shows forth the hidden beauty of God.

2. As I see it, however, we should praise the removal [of attributes] in a way that is contrary to the assertions. For we used to make assertions by beginning from the most valuable and going down through intermediaries to the lowest things. Here, on the other hand, making the ascent from the lowest to the very first, we remove all things in order that we may know without veil that unknowing, which is veiled around by all known things in all existents, and that we may see that transcendent darkness, hidden by light from all that belongs to existing things.

[Commentary]

In the darkness spoken of God is praised by the taking away of all things in the way that has been said; not, however, by the assertions, because then there would not be in that [darkness] the actual unknowing of all things. Outside the darkness, on the other hand, he is praised by both, and principally by the removals; and his praise leads more intimately through the negations to the darkness, and to the unknowing which is in the darkness. Now the author, wishing to clarify this, refers to the approach of praise through the negations (contrary to that which is through the affirmations), saying, *As I see it, however, we should praise the removal [of attributes] in a way that is contrary to the assertions*; meaning, in praising God through the negations to take the opposite way to that which is taken in praise of God through the assertions. *For those indeed* (that is, the assertions) *we used to make*, or we posed, in the way we should have done, *by beginning from the most valuable and going down through the intermediaries to the lowest things*. For in *Theological Representations* he praised God positively, insofar as he is one and three, but in the book *On the Divine Names* he praised him through the intelligible names of God; in the *Symbolic Theology*, however, through descending from the sensible, symbolic naming of God, from the most valuable realities through the middle ones to the very last. *Here, on the other hand*, that is, in the ascent to the peak of the mystical Scriptures, *making the ascent from the lowest*, that is, from sensible things *to the very first, we remove all things in order that we may know without veil that unknowing*, that is, the unknowable

lumine quod in existentibus, hoc est ab omni virtute apprehensiva creata; nulla enim ad eam potest.

CAPITULUM TERTIUM

QUE AFFIRMATIVE THEOLOGIE, QUE ABNEGATIVE

1. In theologicis quidem igitur subfigurationibus principalissima affirmativis theologiis laudavimus, qualiter divina et bona natura unica dicitur, qualiter trina quedam secundum ipsam dicta et paternitas et filiatio, quodcumque est hoc vel quid vult ostendere spiritus theologia, qualiter ex immateriali et impartibili bono precordialia bonitatis exorta sunt lumina, et ab ea que in ipso et in se ipsis et in ad invicem sempiterna germinatione, mansione remanserunt ingressibilia; qualiter supersubstantialis Iesus homini naturalibus veritatibus substantiatur, et quecumque alia ab eloquiis expressa secundum theologicas subfigurationes laudantur, in eo autem quod de divinis nominibus qualiter bonus nominatur, qualiter ens, qualiter vita et sapientia et virtus et quecumque alia intelligibilis sunt dei nominationis, in symbolica autem theologia que a sensibilibus ad divina dei nominationes, que divine forme, que divine figure et membra et organa, que divina loca et ornatus, que ire, que tristitie et insanie, que ebrietates et crapule, que iuramenta et que maledictiones, qui sompni et que vigilie et quecumque alie quaedam sunt symbolice dei figurationis sacreformate formationes.

inaccessibility of the divine light, *which is veiled by all known things in all existents*. For whatsoever is known in any existing thing whatsoever is a veil of that great transcendence, *and that we may see that transcendent darkness*, that is, the same inaccessibility of light, *hidden*, by its very own inaccessibility, of course, *from all that light which is in existents*, that is, from every knowing power that is created; for no such power can attain to him.

CHAPTER III

[Title] WHAT BELONGS TO AFFIRMATIVE THEOLOGY AND WHAT TO NEGATIVE

1. In the *Theological Representations*, therefore, we praised the very first things by affirmative theological expressions: how the divine and good nature is called unique, how it is called threefold; what within it is called fatherhood and sonship, what the theology of the Spirit is and what it wishes to show; how from the immaterial and simple Good the lights in the heart of the Good arose, and in that co-eternal germination have remained without departing from their dwelling in it, as well as in themselves and in each other. And how Jesus, who is beyond particular being, has become a being in the true qualities of human nature. And whatever other things, expressed in the Scriptures, are praised in the *Theological Representations*. In the book *On Divine Names*, on the other hand, in what sense he is called good, in what sense existing, life, wisdom and power, and whatever other things belong to the intelligible naming of God. But in *Symbolic Theology*, what names are taken from the things of sense in the direction of the divine things of God; what the divine forms are; the figures, and the parts and the organs; what the divine places are and what the ornaments; what are the angers, griefs and rage; how is he said to be drunk, and sick with it; and about his oaths and curses; what are his sleepings and wakings, and indeed the other divinely-formed representations which belong to the description of God through symbols.

Capitulum istud est quorundam precedentis capituli declaratio. Primo enim declarat hoc quod dixit: *etenim illas quidem a prestantissimis inchoantes et per media ad ultima descendentes ponebamus*, cuius declarationem breviter tetigimus, et consequenter declarat quod ibi consequitur: *hic autem ab ultimis*. Et ita insimul manifestat quod theologie affirmative, id est per positiones Deum laudantes, sunt Theologice Subfigurationes et ea que De Divinis Nominibus et Symbolica Theologia; abnegative vero sunt que Theologie Mistice. Ait itaque: *in Theologicis quidem igitur Subfigurationibus laudavimus principalissima affirmativis theologiis*, laudando videlicet manifestantes, *qualiter divina et bona natura*, que est *principalissima* et prestantissima, *dicitur unica* seu singularis, *qualiter trina quedam secundum ipsam*, divinam videlicet naturam, *dicta et paternitas et filiatio, quodcumque est hoc vel quid vult ostendere spiritus theologia*: paternitas enim et filiatio et theologia spiritus, quodcumque illa sit, vel quicquid ostendat, trina quedam est secundum divinam naturam, quam trinam, qualiter trina est secundum divinam naturam, declaravit auctor in Theologicis Subfigurationibus; et similiter *qualiter ex immateriali et impartibili bono*, id est ex divina substantia que super omnem materialem compartibilitatem, *exorta sunt* seu germinata sunt, seu explantata sunt, seu edita sunt, *precordialia*, seu si latine diceretur "incordialia," *lumina bonitatis*, hoc est qualiter ex Patre Deo et divina substantia natus est Filius lumen de lumine et processit Spiritus Sanctus similiter lumen de lumine et qualiter, resume, exorta predicto modo lumina *remanserunt germinatione, hoc* est in ipsa germinatione que eterna est, *inegressibilia ab ea mansione sempiterna que in ipso*, bono videlicet immateriali et impartibili, *et in seipsis et in ad invicem*: in eterna enim nativitate Filii et processione Spiritus Sancti utrique sempiterne et inegressibiliter manent in Patre et uterque in seipso et uterque in altero; *qualiter Iesus supersubstantialis* non solum secundum divinitatem sed et secundum humanitatem, sicut dicit beatus Ierotheus, supernaturalis propter unionem humane nature cum divina in eius divina persona, *substantiatur veritatibus naturalibus homini*, hoc est factus est homo verus, integraliter habens et vere homini naturalia; et laudavimus, resume, *quecumque alia ab eloquiis expressa laudantur secundum theologicas subfigurationes*. Laudavit enim in dicto libro ea que invenit in eloquiis expressa tangentia personarum proprietates, quibus ad invicem differunt et characterizantur.

Est autem quod diximus *homini naturalibus* in Greco una dictio composita; quod autem nos transtulimus in nomen *subfigurationis*, hoc est *ypotypωsis*, diversimode potest

[Commentary]

This chapter is a clarification of certain things in the preceding one. First he clarifies this statement which he made: *For we used to make assertions by beginning from the most valuable and going down through intermediaries to the lowest things*; now we have briefly touched upon the clarification of this. He follows on to what comes next: *here, on the other hand, from the lowest*, and thus he shows at the same time that affirmative theology, that is, praising God through affirmations, is *Theological Representations*; and what belongs to *Divine Names* and *Symbolic Theology*. On the other hand, negative theology is the province of *Mystical Theology*. And so he says: *In the Theological Representations, therefore, we praised the very first things by affirmative theological expressions*, meaning: manifesting by praising, *how the divine and good nature* which is *the very first* and the most outstanding, *is called unique* or single, *how it is called threefold, what in it* (meaning the divine nature) *is called fatherhood and sonship, what the theology of the Spirit is and what it wishes to show*. For fatherhood and sonship and the theology of the Spirit (whatever this may be or whatever it may show) is something threefold according to the divine nature, and this Trinity (how it is threefold with regard to the divine nature) the author has clarified in *Theological Representations*, and similarly *how from the immaterial and simple good*, that is, out of the divine substance which is above all material divisibility, *there have arisen*, or there have germinated, or there have been planted out of, or brought out of, *the heart*, or if you could say it in Latin, *incordialia* ["things-in-the-heart"], *the lights of goodness*; that is, how from God the Father and from the divine substance the Son is born, light from light, and how the Holy Spirit has proceeded in a similar way, light from light; and how, in short, the lights which have come forth in the aforesaid manner *have remained in their germination*, that is, in the germination itself which is eternal, *without departing from their dwelling in it*, that is to say, in the immaterial and indivisible good, *as well as in themselves and in each other*; for in the eternal birth of the Son and in the procession of the Holy Spirit both of these [persons] remain eternally in the Father without moving away, and each in himself and each in the other. *How Jesus, who is beyond particular being*, not only in his divinity but also in his humanity (as Bl. Ierotheus says) supernatural because of the union of human nature with the divine in his divine person, *has become a being in the true qualities of human nature*, that is, he has been made a true man, having integrally and truly the natural endowment of man. And (to take up again) we have praised *whatever other things, expressed in the Scriptures, are praised in "Theological Representations."* For in this book he praised the things he has found expressed in the Scriptures touching the properties of the persons, by which they differ from one another and are characterized.

However, what we have put: *homini naturalibus* ["natural endowment of man"] is in Greek a single, composite word. But what we have translated by the noun *subfigurationis*,

transferri;[8] *typos* enim est figura et fixura et character et exemplum et ostensio, unde *typ-cosis* est figuratio et fixio et characterizatio et exemplificatio et ostensio; *ypo* autem prepositio idem est quod "sub," unde *ypotypcosis* potest dici subfiguratio et subfixio et subcharacterizatio et subexemplificatio et subostensio. Existimo autem quod auctor vocet theologicas *ypotypcoseis* divinas proprietates divinas personas distinguentes, et per hoc quasi subcharacterizantes et subfigurantes. *In eo autem* negocio videlicet vel opere *quod De Divinis Nominibus* laudavimus, suple, *qualiter* Deus, suple, *nominatur bonus, qualiter ens, qualiter vita et sapientia et virtus et quecumque alia intelligibilis sunt Dei nominationis*; si enim, ut ibi tactum est, alique intelligibiles Dei nominationes omisse videntur, in dictis ibidem satis explanantur. In *Symbolica autem Theologia* laudavimus, suple, et laudando diximus, *que dei nominationes a sensibilibus ad divina*, hoc est prima significatione significantes sensibilia et per sensibilia significantes spiritalia et divina, et per hoc quasi ascendentes a sensibilibus ad divina; symbolum enim est sensibile aliquid pro intelligibili assumptum, velut pro immateriali et divina cibatione panis et vinum, et quecumque talia: communiter tamen est symbolum omne spiritalioris significativum. Exemplificans autem de symbolicis Dei nominationibus, subiungit: *Que divine forme* corporee videlicet, *que divine figure et membra*, id est partes non habentes proprias distinctas operationes, ut dimidium corporis et huiusmodi, *et organa*, id est partes habentes proprias operationes, ut oculus et auris et huiusmodi, *que divina loca et ornatus*, utpote vestes quibus in scriptura dicitur ornari. Aliqui[9] hic pro "ornatus" dixerunt "mundi"; dictio enim Greca equivoca est ad utrumque. *Que ire, que tristitie, que insanie* seu manie, *que ebrietates et crapule, que iuramenta et que maledictiones, qui sompni et que vigilie et quecumque alie quedam sunt formationes*, corporee videlicet, *sacreformate*, seu sacreplasmate, *Dei figurationis symbolice*. In quibus autem locis et quibus verbis scripture exprimuntur divine forme et figure et membra et cetera omnia que sequuntur, querant illi quibus vacat et qui nihil audent ex scriptura dicere nisi sub ipsis scripture verbis, et qui videri volunt se totam scripturam habere in memorie promptitudine, de quibus est verisimilis coniectura quod, circa sensus scripture vacillantes et egeni, in verborum ipsius copiositate volunt sapientie divitias ostentare.

---

[8] Eriugena: *secundum theologicos characteres*; Sarrazen: *in theologicis hypotyposibus.*
[9] Eriugena.

that is *ypotypωsis*, can be translated in different ways. For *typos* is shape, fixture, character, example and showing — whence *typωsis* is shaping and fixing and characterization and exemplification and showing; *ypo*, on the other hand, is a preposition meaning the same as *sub* ["under"], whence *ypotypωsis* can be rendered sub-shaping and sub-fixing and sub-characterization and sub-exemplification and sub-showing. But I consider that the author will call theological *ypotypωseis* the divine properties distinguishing the divine persons, and in this sense sub-characterizing and sub-figuring. *But in that* discussion or work, he means, *on "Divine Names"* (add: we have praised), *in what sense* (understand: God), *he is called good, in what sense existing, life, wisdom, power, and whatsoever other things belong to the intelligible naming of God.* For if, as was touched on there, some intelligible names of God seem to be omitted, in what is said there they are sufficiently explained. *In "Symbolic Theology"* (add: we have praised, and by praising we have said) *what names are taken from the things of sense in the direction of the divine*, things that through their first reference signify sensible realities, and through sensible realities signify spiritual and divine things; and through this we are ascending, as it were, from sensibles to divine things. For the symbol is something sensible which has been assumed, or has taken the place of, something intelligible; for example, bread and wine for the immaterial and the divine feeding, and whatever is of that order. But in a broader sense a symbol is everything that signifies something more spiritual. But giving an example concerning the symbolic naming of God he adds: *What the divine forms*, meaning corporeal forms, *the figures and parts*, that is, parts not having proper, distinct operations — such as the half of the body, and so on; *and organs*, that is, parts having their own operations, for example the eye, the ear and things like that; *what the divine places are and the ornaments*; for instance, the garments with which he is said in Scripture to be adorned. At this point some have put *mundi* ["worlds"] instead of *ornatus* ["ornaments"], for the Greek word [κόσμοι] is equivocal and can mean both. *What are the angers, griefs and rages* (or madness); *how he is said to be drunk, and sick with it; and about his oaths and curses, what are his sleepings and wakings and indeed other representations* (meaning corporeal forms) *divinely-formed*, or divinely-shaped, *which belong to the description of God through symbols.* However, in what places and by what words of Scripture the divine forms and figures and members and all the other things which follow are expressed — let those [set to work] who have the time, and who dare to say nothing about Scripture except with the very words of Scripture, and who wish to appear to have the whole of Scripture ready in their memory; concerning such there is a probable view to the effect that, being uncertain and poor regarding the senses of Scripture, they want to boast of the riches of their wisdom by means of their fluency in literal quotation.

2. Et te existimo considerasse qualiter multiloquiora magis sunt extrema primis. Etenim oportuit theologicas subfigurationes et divinorum nominum reserationem breviloquiorem esse symbolica theologia, quia quidem, quanto ad superius respicimus, tantum sermones conspectionibus intelligibilium corripiuntur, et quemadmodum et nunc in eam, que super intellectum, ingredientes caliginem, non breviloquium, sed sermonis privationem omnimodam et inintelligibilitatem inveniemus. Et ibi quidem a superiori ad ultima descendens sermo, secundum quantum descensionis ad analogam multitudinem dilatabatur. Nunc autem ab inferioribus ad superpositum ascendens, secundum mensuram ascensionis corripitur, et post omnem ascensionem totus sine voce erit et totaliter unietur ineffabili. Propter quid autem totaliter, ais, a prestantissimo ponentes divinas positiones, ab extremis incipimus divinam ablationem? Quoniam quod super omnem ponentes positionem a magis ipsi cognatiori suppositivam affirmationem oportuit ponere: quod autem super omnem ablationem auferentes, a magis ab ipso distantibus auferre. Vel nonne magis est vita et bonitas quam aer et lapis, et magis non crapule et non insanie quam non dicitur neque intelligitur?

Ostenso secundum que laudatur et quod affirmative laudatur Deus in tribus predictis negotiis, adicit quod inferiora, utpote symbolica, sunt plurium sermonum quam superiora et secundum analogiam superioritatis est abreviatio sermonis. Inferiora enim et sensibilia sunt compositiora superioribus et intelligibilibus et propter hoc pluribus indigent sermonibus in sue totalitatis ostensionem et in symbolice significatorum declarationem. Alloquens itaque Timotheum, ait: *Et existimo te*, o Timothee, *considerasse* seu conspexisse, *qualiter multiloquiora magis*, id est plurium locutionum et sermonum, magis *sunt extrema primis*, id est sensibilia intelligibilibus. *Etenim oportuit Theologicas Subfigurationes et Divinorum Nominum reserationem breviloquiorem esse Symbolica Theologia, quia quidem quanto ad superius respicimus, tantum sermones conspectionibus intelligibilium*

2. I think you have been able to reflect on how it is that the last things are expressed in more words than the first. For it was necessary that the *Theological Representations* and the disclosure of the *Divine Names* should be briefer than the *Symbolic Theology*. The reason is, that the more we look to the higher, the more the words are contracted by our glances at the intelligible things. So that now, as we enter into darkness which is beyond the mind, we shall find not brevity in words but perfect irrationality and unwisdom. In the other case, indeed, the discourse went downward from the highest things to the lowest, and it was widened out to an extent proportional to the quantity of descent. At present, ascending from the lower things to the highest, it is contracted according to the measure of the ascent. And after the whole ascent [the discourse] will be completely voiceless, and will be united wholly to the One who is beyond discourse. But you say: why should we have started from the absolutely first when laying down positive statements about the divine? Why do we make the taking away [of attributes] from the divine begin from the lowest? The reason is that because [the First] is beyond every assertion, those who are making an affirmation that is more than affirmation, had to base the assertion on what is more cognate to the First. When we are removing that which is above all it was necessary to make the removal [of attributes] from him starting from the more distant things. Or is he not rather life and goodness than air and stone? And is he not further from being sickness and madness than from not lying within speech and understanding?

[Commentary]

Having shown in what respect God is praised, and that God is praised affirmatively in the three foregoing treatises, he adds that the lower things as symbolic entities take longer to characterize than do the higher things, and according to the measure of superiority the discourse is shortened. For inferior and sensible things are more composite than superior and intelligible ones, and for that reason they need more words to show them forth in the wholeness of what they are, and to clarify what they mean symbolically. And thus, addressing Timothy he says, *And I think you*, Timothy, *have been able to reflect on* (or to have seen) *how it is that in more words*, that is, more expressions and words, *the last things are [expressed] rather than the first*, that is, the things of sense than the intelligibles. *For it was necessary that the "Theological Representations" and the*

corripiuntur; superiora enim secundum analogiam sue superioritatis simplificantur, et propter hoc eorum intelligentie minus numerose et per consequens sermones qui significant eorum intellectus pauciores. Et cum ascendendo supergressi fuerimus in creatis simplicissima, non erit breviloquium sed omnimoda sermonis privatio, quemadmodum et in mistica theologia ingredientes caliginem, omnimodam sermonis et intelligentie habent privationem. Unde sequitur: *et quemadmodum et nunc*, id est in mistica theologia, *ingredientes in eam caliginem que super intellectum, non breviloquium sed sermonis privationem*, seu si latine diceretur, "illocutionem," *omnimodam et inintelligibilitatem* seu inintelligentiam, hoc est non intelligentiam, *inveniemus. Et ibi quidem*, id est in theologia affirmativa que est in tribus predictis negotiis, *sermo descendens a superiori ad ultima*, hoc est a summis creaturis gradatim ad infima, *dilatabatur secundum quantum*, id est secundum quantitatem, *descensionis ad multitudinem analogam*, id est comproportionalem, descensioni videlicet. *Nunc autem*, id est in mistica theologia, *ascendens*, sermo videlicet per abnegationes, *ab inferioribus ad superpositum, corripitur*, id est abreviatur, *secundum mensuram ascensionis, et post omnem ascensionem* per ordinatam abnegationem omnium ab infimis ad suprema *totus*, sermo videlicet, id est tota vis sermocinativa tam sermone intus disposito quam exterius prolato, *sine voce*, seu si latine diceretur, "invocus" *erit, et totaliter unietur ineffabili.*

Et quia et in precedenti capitulo et hic dixit auctor quod in laude Dei et doctrina laudis eius per positiones et affirmativas theologias descendit sermo ordinatius a prestantissimis per media ad ultima, et in laude et doctrina laudis eius per ablationes et abnegativas theologias ascendit sermo ab ultimis ad principalissima, nec huius contrarie incessionis assignavit rationem, inducit Timotheum querentem huius contrarie incessionis rationem, quam assignat talem. Quoniam laudantes eum, qui super positionem omnium, per positiones et quasi unam laudis eius integritatem componentes et edificantes, oportet a cognatioribus et proximioribus ipsi incipere et sic gradatim descendere usque ad ultima, quemadmodum natura componens et edificans corpus animalis organicum post cor incipit a proximioribus cordi, sic gradatim procedens usque ad extrema; querentes autem quod intimum est in multis circumpositis ipsi et ipsum occultantibus, oportet primo auferre ultima et sic gradatim auferre donec perveniatur ad ipsi proxima, ut illis tandem ablatis denudetur et inveniatur quesitum, quemadmodum faciunt naturale agalma, ut interiori ligni vel lapidis querentes primo auferunt exteriora, et sic consequenter usque perveniunt ad intimum naturale agalma. Ordinata igitur incessio componentium aliquid est, post positum et primum et fundamentum, a proximioribus ipsi

disclosure of the "Divine Names" should be briefer than the "Symbolic Theology." The reason is, that the more we look to the higher, the more the words are contracted by our glances at the intelligible things. For the superior things are simplified in the measure of their superiority, and for that reason insights into them are less numerous, and as a consequence the words which signify the understanding of them are fewer. And when in our ascent we shall have made our way above the most simple of created things there shall be no short word but a total privation of the word, insofar as in *Mystical Theology* those who are entering the darkness are completely deprived of word and insight. Whence it follows: *So that now,* that is, in *Mystical Theology, as we enter into that darkness which is beyond the mind it is not brevity in words but absence of words,* or, if it could be said in Latin *illocutionem* ["non-locution"], *totally, and unintelligibility* (or non-intelligibility, that is, no intelligence) *that we shall find. In the other case, indeed,* that is, in affirmative theology (which consists in the three treatises referred to) *the discourse went downwards from the highest things to the lowest,* that is, from the highest creatures step by step to the lowest; *it was widened out in proportion to the quantity,* that is, according to the quantity *of descent, on analogous scale,* that is, to the descent. *At present* (meaning, in *Mystical Theology) ascending* (referring to the discourse through negations) *from the lower things to the highest it is contracted,* that is to say, it is abbreviated, *according to the measure of the ascent. And after the whole ascent* through the coordinated negation of all things, from the lowest to the highest, *the whole* (meaning, the whole word, that is, the whole speech power, in terms both of the word which is framed interiorly and the word that is brought forth exteriorly,) *will be voiceless,* or if it could be said in Latin *invocus* ["non-voiced"], *and will be united totally to the One beyond discourse.*

Now because the author has said, both in the preceding chapter and here, that in the praise of God and the teaching of his praise through the assertions and the affirmative theologies, the discourse descends in a more orderly way from the most outstanding things through the middle to the last; and in the praise, and the teaching of the praise, of God through the removal [of attributes] and the negative theologies the discourse mounts upwards from the last to the absolutely first, and he has not [yet] given a reason for this contrary direction, he brings in Timothy asking the reason for this contrary approach. The reason he gives is the following. For we, praising him who is above the positing of all things through the positive terms, and, as it were, composing and building up a single whole of his praise, must begin from the things that are more cognate and closer to him, and thus, step by step, go right down to the last things (an example: nature, when it is putting together and building up the organic body of an animal begins, after the heart, with the things closest to the heart and thus, level by level, proceeds right down to the last things): we, as we seek what is at the core of the many things which are placed around him and which hide him, have first to take away the last things, and so, level by level, to remove things until we come to what is closest to him, in order

incipere et procedere per eorum media usque ad magis distantia; querentium vero primum et fundamentum et intimum adhuc eis occultum, ordinata incessio est predicte incessioni contraria. Inducens igitur Timotheum querentem, ait: *propter quid autem, ais*, mihi videlicet, o Timothee, *ponentes divinas positiones totaliter a prestantissimo*, inchoantes, suple, *incipimus ab extremis* seu ultimis *divinam ablationem*? Et subiungens rationem quesiti, ait: *quoniam ponentes*, quasi primum videlicet et fundamentum, *quod super omnem positionem, oportuit ponere* et ponendo componere *suppositivam*, id est subiunctivam et consequentem, *affirmationem* laudis videlicet ipsius; *a magis ipsi cognatiori auferentes autem*, id est per ablationem laudantes et querentes, *quod super omnem ablationem* oportuit, resume, *auferre a magis ab ipso distantibus*, quemadmodum et iste auctor fecit; laudans ipsum positive, incepit a prestantissimis, hoc est ab ydiomatibus characteristicis personarum in Theologicis Subfigurationibus, continuans per ordinem suum incessum per intelligibiles nominationes divinas significantes beneficos eius processus ad creaturas in Divinis Nominibus, et sic descendens ad sensibilia et extrema ipsum symbolice significantia in Symbolica Theologia; hic autem, querens ipsum ut intimum omnium per abnegationes omnium ab ipso, primo amovet ab ipso sensibilia tamquam ab ipso magis distantia, et deinde intelligibilia tamquam ipsi proximiora. Post rationem itaque redditam Timotheo contrarie incessionis in ablationibus et positionibus divinis, manifestat Timotheo per exemplum a se dictorum se in laude divina et eius quesitione dictam rationem secutum esse. Quasi igitur diceret Timotheo: Hanc rationem tibi querenti redditam secutus sum, adiungit in eius ostensionem: *vel nonne magis est vita et bonitas*, de quibus videlicet dixi in libro De Divinis Nominibus, *quam aer et lapis*, de quibus subsequenter dixi in Simbolica Theologia? Si autem magis sunt, et ipsi, qui per se est et a nullo est, proximiores et cognatiores sunt, et ita processit meus sermo positive laudativus a cognatioribus et proximioribus ad elongatiora. Et nonne, resume, *non crapule et non insanie*, seu non manie, magis distantium videlicet sunt abnegationes, *quam non dicitur neque intelligitur*, immo vero magis distantium sunt abnegationes; propinquior enim est Deo dictio et intelligentia quam crapula et insania, quarum prior est ex concupiscentia, altera ex ira, et prius abnegantes auferimus eas a Deo in proximo capitulo sequente, dicentes quod non habet turbationem a passionibus materialibus perturbatus, quam abnegamus ab eo dici et intelligi cum dicimus in ultimo capitulo: *neque dicitur neque intelligitur*, et sic rationem tibi redditam secuti sumus. Si autem alicui videtur quasi coacta suppletio quam fecimus post hanc dictionem "magis" secundo positam, et sic solum ex vi littere esse supplendum: *et nonne magis est vel sunt non crapule* et cetera, non contendimus cum eo; sed si concedit distantioris abnegationem prius esse natura et ita *magis* esse quam abnegationem propinquioris, libenter ei annuimus.

that when finally they are removed the one who is sought may be stripped naked and be found. (An example: when they make a natural image of something, those who are seeking what lies inside the wood or the stone first take away all that is around it, and continue until they reach the natural image which lies within.) Therefore the orderly approach of the things making up something is, after the thing positively identified, the factor that comes first and that is the foundation: to begin from the things that are closest to it and to proceed through the intermediary things right down to the things that are further from it. But in the case of those who are seeking the First and the foundation and the very core which remains still hidden to them, the orderly way of procedure is contrary to the approach which has been outlined. And therefore, bringing in Timothy with a question, he says *But why, you say* (meaning to me), Timothy, *should we* (have started, that is) *from the absolutely first, when laying down positive statements about the divine, only to begin from the lowest*, or the very last things, *when removing divine attributes?* Giving the answer to this question he says, *Since those who are affirming* (meaning: as the [absolutely] first and the foundation) *what is beyond all affirmation had to affirm* (and by affirming to form) *a related*, that is, annexed and consequent *affirmation* (meaning: in praise of him) [based upon] *what is more cognate to him. On the other hand those removing*, that is, those praising and seeking through taking away, *that which is above every removal* (add: had to) *make the removal starting from things more distant*; just as this author has done: praising God positively, he began from the most outstanding things, that is, from the properties which characterize the persons in theological representations, continuing his orderly approach through intelligible divine nominations signifying his providential outgoing toward creatures, in *Divine Names*; and thus descending to sensible things and last things, which signify God symbolically, in *Symbolic Theology*. But here, on the other hand, seeking [God] as the most intimate of all things through the taking away of all [attributes] from him, he first removes from him sensible things, as being at a greater distance from him, and then intelligible things, as being closer to him. And so, after giving this reason to Timothy for the contrary direction of approach in the divine negations and in the divine affirmations, he shows Timothy, through the example of the things said by him, that in praise of God and in the search for him he has applied the aforesaid method. It is as though he were to say to Timothy: I have followed this reason that has been given to you in answer to your question. And to show that he adds: *Or is he not rather life and goodness* (concerning which, of course, I have spoken in the book of *Divine Names*) *than air and stone?* (about which I have subsequently spoken in *Symbolic Theology*.) If, however, they are rather more close and more cognate with the nature of him who is through himself and who is underived from any other, then my discourse, praising through affirming, has proceeded [by starting] from the more cognate and closer things [and moving] in the direction of those further off. And (add) *is he not further from being sickness and madness?*

Et advertendum quod non reprobat auctor iste ascensionem ab infimis creaturis per media usque ad supremas in laude Dei et quesitione eius per positiones omnium: ascendunt enim sic per ordinem operationes virtutum speculativarum, et est hec ascensio cum Moyse et sacerdotibus usque ad montis verticem. Sed compositio doctrinalis unius et integre laudis divine per omnium positiones ordinatius et naturalius procedit a primis et Deo cognatioribus usque ad infima, quesitio vero eius per omnium abnegationes ordinatius et naturalius procedit ab infimis per media usque ad summa, et necesse est sive positive sive ablative ascendentes ab infimis per media usque ad summa, antequam intrent caliginem, omnia totaliter ab ipso, qui queritur, abnegare, et omnia sive positive sive abnegative inventa transcendere, et ab omnium conspectione quiescere et sic fieri in caligine.

CAPITULUM QUARTUM

QUONIAM NIHIL SENSIBILIUM QUI OMNIS SENSIBILIS SECUNDUM SUPEREXCELLENTIAM CAUSA

Dicamus igitur quod omnium causa et super omnes existens et neque sine substantia est neque sine vita, neque sine ratione, neque sine intellectu, neque corpus est, neque figura, neque species, neque qualitatem vel

(or: he is not madness): these are negations of things that are more distant (he means) *than not lying within speech and understanding*; indeed, they are the negations of things which are more distant. For speech and intelligence are closer to God than debauch and madness, of which the first comes from concupiscence and the second from anger. First in our negations we remove them from God (in the next chapter following) saying that he does not suffer through disturbance by material passions, before negating speech and intelligence in his regard, when we say in the last chapter: *nor is he spoken nor understood*. Thus we have followed the method that has been given in answer to you. But if it seems to someone that what we have added after the word *more* (second occurrence) is somewhat forced, so that there should be added only (following the thrust of the text) *and is (or are) not being sickness not further from him?* (and so on), we will have no quarrel with him. If, on the other hand, he concedes that the negation of the more distant quality is prior in nature and thus is *more*, rather than the negation of what is closer, then we will freely agree with him.

Now it should be noted that this author does not condemn the ascent from the lowest creatures up through the intermediary to the highest in the praise of God and in the seeking of him, by means of the affirmation of all things; because the operations of the speculative virtues ascend thus in an order, and this is the ascent with Moses and the priests right up to the summit of the mountain. But the doctrinal composition of one total divine praise through the affirmation of all things proceeds in a more orderly way and more naturally from the first things, which also are the closest to God, right down to the last things; while, on the other hand, the seeking of him through the negations of all things proceeds in a more orderly and a more natural way from the last things up through the middle to the highest. And it is necessary, whether they are ascending through positive attributions or by means of removing [the attributes] from the lowest things through the intermediary right up to the highest, that before they enter the darkness they must totally deny all things of him who is the object of the search, and must transcend all that they have found whether positive or negative; and they have to rest from the sight of all and thus enter the darkness.

CHAPTER IV

[Title] THE CAUSE OF EVERY SENSIBLE THING WHICH IS BEYOND CAUSE IS NOTHING OF THE SENSIBLE THINGS

1. Let us say therefore that the cause of all things, existing beyond all, is neither without a substance, nor without life, nor without reason, nor without mind; it is not a body, nor a shape, nor a form; it has neither quality

quantitatem vel tumorem habet, neque in loco est, neque videtur, neque tactum sensibilem habet, neque sentitur, neque sensibilis est, neque inordinationem habet et turbationem, a passionibus materialibus perturbata, neque impotens est, sensibilibus subiecta symptomatibus, neque in indigentia est luminis, neque alterationem vel corruptionem vel particionem vel privationem neque aliud quid sensibilium neque est, neque habet.

Quia ascensus in caliginem ubi vere est Deus, et ubi secretissima est cum Deo locutio et mistica theologia, que maxime est visio et cognitio quod ipse est invisibilis et incognoscibilis, principalius est per abnegationes omnium ab infimis per media usque ad summa, in fine sermonis De Mistica Theologia, de qua secundum se non potest plus dici quam quod est sine dictione et sermone, pertinenter vero ad illam non potest dici nisi aptitudo ascensurorum, de qua iam dictum est, et gradus et ordo ascensionum, manifestat gradus et ordinem ascensionum per abnegationem omnium, primo sensibilium et consequenter intelligibilium. Sed ne ex abnegatione omnium a Deo posset quis opinari auctorem intendere dicere Deum omnino non esse, premittit eum esse supersubstantialiter substantiam, vitam, rationem et intellectum, qui tamen simpliciter [et] essentialiter nihil est entium vel non entium. Ait itaque: *Dicamus igitur quod omnium causa et existens super omnes*, seu super omnia, *et neque sine substantia est, neque sine vita, neque sine ratione, neque sine intellectu*, seu si latine diceretur, "et neque insubstantialis est, neque invitalis, neque irrationalis, neque inintellectualis"; est enim hec, sed ut dictum est, supersubstantialiter et superessentialiter; dicamus, inquam, quod illa causa *neque corpus est*, quod consideratum ut corpus infima rerum est et a Deo distantissima, cui proximum est ascendendo corpus figuratum; corpus enim unde corpus est quantum, ad quod proximo sequitur figuratum, et huic proximum corpus aliqua forma naturali specificatum, et consequenter accidentibus speciei convenientibus qualificatum, ad que sequitur quod sit quantum quantitate determinata perfecta conveniente speciei secundum tres dimensiones. Hec itaque habet corpus secundum dictum ordinem meliorationis et appropinquationis ad optimum ex parte sui; ex parte autem exteriorum sensibilium, primo locatum est et ubi, cum quo cointelligitur in tempore et quando, deinde sentitur, primo visu et consequenter aliis sensibus. Si autem transcendat naturas corporeas carentes vita, post vegetabile fit sensitivum et habet irascibile et concupiscibile et ex hiis perturbationem, et subiectum sensibilium discrasiis, fit egrotans et impotens et deficiens secundum virtutes sensitivas et alteratum et corruptum, et post corruptionem in ea ex quibus componitur resolutum et partitum et privatum hiis quibus ex compositione participabat. Hec itaque sic naturaliter secundum ascensum ordinata, sensibus sunt subiecta. Videtur autem quod auctor hic omiserit naturam vegetativam, que media est

nor quantity or weight; it is not in place nor is it seen; it does not have sensible touch nor can it be felt, nor is it a sensible thing; it does not suffer from disorder or disturbance coming from the material passions, nor is it powerless or subject to sensible events, nor is it in need of light, nor does it have variation or corruption or division or privation, or any other sensible thing; it neither is nor has any of these.

[Commentary]

Since the ascent into the darkness where God truly is and where there is the most secret speaking with God, and mystical theology, which is in the highest degree the vision and the knowledge that he is invisible and unknowable, consist ultimately rather more in the negation of all, from the lowest through the intermediary right up to the highest, at the end of the discourse *On Mystical Theology* (concerning which, taken in itself, no more can be said than that it is without word and without discourse, but with reference to it nothing can be said unless concerning the preparedness of those about to ascend, which has already been done, and the steps and the order of the ascents), he brings to light the grades and the order of the ascents through the negation of all things, first of sensible things and following that of intelligible things. But lest someone should take the view, based on the negation of all [attributes] in respect of God, that the author intends to say that God does not exist at all, he states at the beginning that God is supersubstantially substance, life, reason and intellect; however, he simply and essentially is nothing of the things that are, or of the things that are not. And thus he says: *Let us say, therefore, that the cause of all things, existing beyond all* (or all things) *is neither without substance, nor without life, nor without reason, nor without understanding*, or, if that were said in Latin, *et neque insubstantialis est, neque invitalis, neque irrationalis, neque inintellectualis.* For he is these things; but, as was remarked, in a manner that is beyond being and essence. Let us say (I remark) that that cause *is not a body*, which, considered as body, is the lowest of all things and the thing furthest from God. The next thing to that (moving upwards) is body with shape; for body, insofar as it is body, is a quantity, and upon that there follows in the next place shape. And the next body to that is specified by some natural form. The next following upon that has quality through the accidents befitting the species. It follows upon that again that it should be a quantity [but with] determinate quantity that is complete, and fitting three-dimensionally to the species. These things body possesses according to the aforesaid order of improvement and of approaching to what is best, taken in itself. But from the side of exterior, sensible things, on the other hand, first is being placed, and where; with that is co-understood being in time, and when; after that it is sensed, first by sight and then by the other senses. If, however, it transcends the corporeal natures that lack life, after vegetable it

inter corpora penitus carentia vita et corpora sensitiva. Sed potest dici quod per extrema dedit intelligi medium, sicut pluries faciunt philosophice tractantes. Si autem dicat quis quod ea que dicta sunt post hoc corpus sensitivum non addunt corpori sensitivo meliorationem et appropinquationem ad optimum, respondendum ei quod si preter naturam corporis sensitivi adessent corpori sensitivo, vere diceret; sed quia secundum naturam corporis sensitivi assunt ei, et omne quod secundum naturam est, bonum est, dicto ordine advenientia corpori sensitivo addunt ad meliorationem et ad proximationem ad optimum.

Itaque secundum dictum ordinem ascensionis sensibilium, abnegans ea auctor ab omnium causa, ponens pro plerisque concretis cum corpore eorum abstracta, ait de ea *quoniam neque corpus est neque figura neque species*, hoc est neque corpus figuratum neque specificatum, *neque qualitatem habet vel quantitatem*, longitudinis videlicet et latitudinis, vel *tumorem*, hoc est profunditatem, quia nec est corpus qualificatum nec quantitate determinata quantum, *neque in loco est, neque videtur, neque tactum sensibilem habet*, quia non tangitur, *neque sentitur*, aliquo videlicet sensuum medio inter visum et tactum, *neque sensibilis est*, quia nec est, nec habet animam sensibilem nec organa sensitiva, *neque inordinationem habet et turbationem perturbata a passionibus materialibus*, id est a concupiscentia et ira et earum speciebus, *neque subiecta sensibilibus symptomatibus*, id est coaccidentibus discrasiis ex contrarietate componentium vel in tempore circumstantium, [neque] *est impotens* per debilitationem ex egritudine, *neque est in indigentia luminis*, per defectionem videlicet sensuum quinque exteriorum, quorum quilibet est activus per corporale lumen in eo vigens, *neque habet alterationem vel corruptionem vel particionem vel privationem*, ut predictum est, *neque est neque habet aliud quid sensibilium*.

becomes sensitive and has the irascible and concupiscible powers, and from these it has disturbance and is subject to the warring qualities of sensible things, it becomes ill and powerless and deficient with regard to the sensitive powers, and altered and corrupted; and after its corruption into those things of which it is composed it is dissolved, and broken into parts, and deprived of those things, coming from composition, in which it participated. That is how these things, ordained by nature in an upward development, are subjected to the senses. It appears, however, that the author has omitted here the vegetative nature, which comes in between bodies that completely lack life and sensitive bodies. But it can be said that through the extremes he has given to understand what is intermediary, as those who are conducting a philosophical inquiry frequently do. But if the objection were made that these things which were mentioned after sensitive body do not add to the sensitive body improvement and approximation to the best, the reply must be made that if they were present in the sensitive body over and beyond the nature of the sensitive body then what he says would be true, but since they are present in it because of the [very] nature of sensitive body, and since all that is according to nature is good, the features that supervene in the aforesaid order upon the sensitive body add to it improvement, and to its approximation to what is best.

And so, according to the order that has been laid out of the ascent by means of sensible things, the author, denying these in respect of the cause of all things, and putting abstract [terms] for most of the concrete things with their bodies, says of it *that it is not a body nor a shape or form*, that is, neither a body with shape or within a species, *it has neither quality nor quantity* (meaning: length or breadth,) *or swelling*, that is, depth, because he is neither body with qualities nor a quantity of a determinate kind. *It is not in place nor is it seen; it does not have sensible touch* because it is not touched, *nor can it be felt*, that is to say, by one of the senses that is intermediary between sight and touch; *nor is it a sensible thing*, because it neither is nor has a sensible soul or sense organs; *it does not suffer from disorder and disturbance coming from the material passions*, that is, from concupiscence and anger and their [various] species; *nor is it subject to sensible events*, that is, to the warring qualities that come about from the opposed nature of the components, or of temporal circumstances; *nor is it powerless* through debilitation resulting from illness; *nor is it in need of light*, through not having the five external senses, of which each one is active through the corporeal light which thrives in it, *nor does it have variation or corruption or division or privation*. As was said: *it neither is nor has any sensible thing*.

CAPITULUM QUINTUM

QUONIAM NIHIL INTELLIGIBILIUM QUI OMNIS INTELLIGIBILIS SECUNDUM SUPEREXCELLENTIAM CAUSA

Rursus autem ascendentes dicamus quod neque anima est, neque intellectus, neque fantasiam vel opinionem vel rationem vel intelligentiam habet, neque ratio est, neque intelligentia, neque dicitur, neque intelligitur, neque numerus est, neque ordo, neque magnitudo, neque parvitas, neque equalitas,[10] neque similitudo, neque dissimilitudo, neque stat, neque movetur, neque silencium ducit, neque habet potentiam, neque potentia est neque lumen, neque vivit, neque vita est, neque substantia est, neque seculum, neque tempus, neque tactus est ipsius intelligibilis, neque scientia, neque veritas est, neque regnum, neque sapientia, neque unum, neque unitas, neque deitas vel bonitas, neque spiritus est, ut nos scire, neque filiatio, neque paternitas, neque aliud quid nobis vel alii alicui entium cognitorum, neque quid non entium, neque quid entium est, neque entia ipsam noscunt secundum quod ipsa est, neque ipsa cognoscit entia secundum quod entia sunt, neque ratio ipsius est, neque nomen, neque cognitio, neque tenebra est, neque lumen, neque error, neque veritas, neque est ipsius universaliter positio neque ablatio, sed eorum que post ipsam positiones et ablationes facientes, ipsam neque ponimus, neque auferimus, quia et super omnem positionem est omnino perfecta et unitiva omnium causa, et super omnem ablationem superexcellentia ab omnibus simpliciter absoluti et ultra universa.

Procedens auctor ascendendo a sensibilibus ad intelligibilia, et in ipsis intelligibilibus ab inferioribus ad superiora, cum intelligibiles substantie non sint nisi anima, que inferior est et a Deo distantior, et angelus qui superior, supra quem non est substantia creata nec Deo proximior, licet in angelis multi sint ordines inferiores et superiores, abnegat primo a prima omnium causa ipsam esse animam, et deinde ipsam esse angelum. Et quia melior est omnis res in suo actu naturali naturaliter se habens quam in se nude

---

[10] Grosseteste did not translate the next two words of the Greek text: οὔτε ἀνισότης ("or inequality").

CHAPTER V

[Title] THAT THE TRANSCENDENT CAUSE OF EVERY INTELLIGIBLE REAL-
ITY IS NOT ONE OF THE INTELLIGIBLE REALITIES

1. As we ascend again let us say that it is not soul nor intellect; nor has
it imagination or opinion, nor reason or intelligence — it is not reason or
intelligence; it is not spoken, it is not understood; it is not number or
order, nor greatness or smallness, nor equality; nor similarity or dissimilarity; it neither stays at rest nor is it moved; nor does it bring about silence
or have power; nor is it power or light; it does not live nor is it life; it is
not substance, or everlastingness, or time; it cannot be grasped by the
understanding; it is not knowledge or truth; nor kingship or wisdom; it
is neither one nor unity, nor deity or goodness. It is not Spirit in the sense
that we understand that, nor sonship or fatherhood, nor anything that is
known by us or by any other being; nor is it anything among non-existents or among existents; nor do existents know it as it itself is; nor does
it know existing things as such; there is no expression of it or name or
knowledge; it is not darkness and it is not light, it is not error and it is
not truth; it is completely beyond any assertion or any taking away; when
we make assertions or take away [attributes derived] from those things that
come after it, we neither assert nor remove anything concerning it, since
beyond every assertion it is the perfect and uniting cause of all things, and
it transcends all taking away by virtue of its simple and absolute nature
beyond all things.

[Commentary]

The author proceeds on the way upwards from sensible things to intelligible things,
and among the intelligible things themselves from the lower to the higher. Since the only
intelligible substances are the soul, which is lower and more distant from God, and the
angel, which is higher, above which there is no created substance nor anything closer to
God (even though among the angels there are many lower and higher orders,) in respect
of the first cause of all things he denies first that it is a soul and then that it is an angel.
Now since everything is better in its own natural act than when considered abstractly
in itself; and the operations of the soul are imagination, opinion, and reason actually at

considerate; anime autem operationes sunt ymaginatio, opinio, ratio actu ratiocinans; angeli vero, qui est intellectus, operatio naturalis est intelligentia; dicit consequenter abnegando, primam causam nec esse animam naturaliter operantem, nec angelum naturaliter operantem, abnegans ab ipsa ipsas naturales utriusque operationes. Et quia operatio naturalis que efficit operantem meliorem melior est operante, abnegat consequenter omnium causam esse anime et angeli operationem. Et quia intelligibile est melius intelligente, ut patet ex dictis in Divinis Nominibus, et similiter dicibile et summum quod dici potest melius dicente, abnegat consequenter a causa omnium, tanquam excelsius et sibi propinquius anima et angelo naturaliter operantibus et earum naturalibus operationibus, dicibile per anime rationem et intelligibile per angeli intelligentiam. Nec est quo superius potest secundum hanc viam a sensibilibus per intelligibilia solum procedi: posset tamen ascensus iste incomparabiliter multiplicius dici, utpote si, cum pervenitur ad angelum, divideretur in ordines angelicos et secundum ascensus ordinum enarrarentur ascensiones abnegationum, et similiter in ceteris.

Has igitur ascensiones abnegativas manifestans auctor ait: *Rursus autem ascendentes dicamus quod neque anima est*, ipsa videlicet omnium causa, *neque intellectus*, id est neque angelus, consuete enim vocat auctor iste angelum "intellectum," *neque habet fantasiam, id est ymaginationem, vel opinionem vel rationem*, agentes videlicet ut per has sit anima naturaliter agens, *vel intelligentiam*, que est actio intellectus ut per hanc sit intellectus agens, *neque est ratio, neque intelligentia, neque dicitur* verbo videlicet rationis, *neque intelligitur* actione intellectus agentis. Iste igitur est ascensus a sensibilibus per intelligibilia solum.

Sunt autem que comuniter assunt sensibilibus et intelligibilibus, que in sensibilibus sensu sunt perceptibilia et maxime sensu rationi counito, in intelligibilibus vero solo intellectu, et similiter nude in se et abstracte considerata, solo intellectu sunt apprehensibilia. Hec autem sunt numerus, qui omnem rem, simul ac est, consequitur, et quies et motus, quorum alterum necessario consequitur cuiusque rei exsistentiam, secundum quod omne agens moveri dicitur et non agens quiescere, et potentia naturalis, que similiter omnem rem consequitur, et mensura essendi, qua res omnis necessario participat, et appetitus boni, qui naturaliter inest omni rei. A sensibilibus igitur et intelligibilibus potest procedi ad hec quibus omnia participant, et in horum singulo ascendi per ea que ipsa ordinate bonificant. Post ascensum igitur per sensibilia et intelligibilia solum, transit auctor ad omnibus communia et primo ad numerum, abnegans eum ab omnium causa et dicens: *neque numerus est*; et quia numerum necessario immediate consequitur ordo, qui bonificat numerum et numerata, sine ordine enim non est nisi horror et perturbatio, continuo adiungit: *neque ordo*; et quia ordo est parium dispariumque rerum

work; and since the natural operation of the angel (which is an intellect) is intelligence, he goes on as a consequence to deny that the first cause is either a soul naturally operating or an angel operating according to its nature: he denies of it the natural operations of either. And since a natural operation which renders the agent better is better than the agent, he denies in consequence that the first cause of all things is the operation of the soul and the angel. And because the intelligible is better than the one understanding, as is clear from what was said in *Divine Names*; and similarly something that is sayable and the highest that can be said is better than the one speaking, he goes on to deny in regard to the cause of all things that it is sayable through the reason of the soul and intelligible through the intelligence of the angel, as the highest thing and closer to itself than the soul and the angel working naturally and their natural operations. And now there is no higher place where, on the line of this road from sensible things to intelligible things alone, he can proceed. Yet that ascent could be expressed in an incomparably more differentiated manner if, for instance, when he arrives at the angel, it were to be divided up into the angelic orders, and the ascending movements of negation were spelt out according to the ascending orders; and similarly in other things.

Bringing to light, therefore, these rising movements of negation the author says *As we ascend again let us say that it is not soul*, meaning: the cause of all things, *or intellect*, that is, not an angel (for this author habitually calls the angel "intellect"); *nor has it fantasia, that is, imagination; or opinion or reason*, meaning: these powers acting so that through them the soul is acting naturally; *or intelligence*, which is the action of the intellect that makes the latter an agent intellect; *it is not reason or intelligence, it is not spoken*, meaning: by the word of the reason; *it is not understood* by the action of the agent intellect. That, therefore, is the ascent from sensible things to intelligible things alone.

There are, however, things which belong to sensible and intelligible realities taken in common, which in the sensible things are perceptible by sense, and especially by sense united to reason, and on the other hand in intelligible things by the intellect alone, and similarly, nakedly in themselves and abstractly considered, are apprehensible by the intellect alone. These, however, are number, which follows upon everything as soon as it is there; and rest and motion, one of which follows necessarily upon the existence of each thing, insofar as every agent is said to be moved and every non-acting thing is said to rest; and natural power, which similarly belongs to everything; and the measure of being in which everything necessarily shares; and the love of the good which is naturally within everything. There could, therefore, be a way of proceeding from sensible and intelligible things to those realities in which all participate, and it would be possible to ascend in an orderly way in each one of these through those beings which confer on them the good. Therefore, after the ascent through sensible and intelligible things alone, the author passes to what is common to all, and first to number, denying it of the cause of

sua cuique tribuens loca dispositio,[11] necessario in ordine est maioritas quocumque modo prioritatis et minoritas quocumque modo posterioritatis posteriorum et equalitas parium, et per hoc necessario similitudo et dissimilitudo, que omnia sunt de ordinis perfectione et bonitate; que consequenter abnegans ab omnium causa, ait: *neque magnitudo*, dicta videlicet a maioritate prioritatis in ordine, *neque parvitas*, dicta videlicet a minoritate posterioritatis in ordine, *neque equalitas* in ordine parium, *neque similitudo* equalium, *neque dissimilitudo* disparium: omnium enim causa nullum horum est.

Et quia supra rerum ordinem non est quo superius ascendatur, ordo enim omnia pacificat,[12] revertitur auctor ad motum et quietem que sub disiunctione sequuntur ad omnia, abnegans utrumque ab omnium causa: quietem tamen oppositam motui consequenti ad omnia, dividit in stationem que est privatio actionis et motionis sensibilis, et in silencium, quod est privatio actionis et motionis intelligibilis: non enim agunt intelligibilia nisi verbo intelligibili. Abnegans igitur utrumque, id est quietem et motum, ab omnium causa, ait: *neque stat, neque movetur, neque silencium ducit*. Supra quietem autem et motum sic generaliter dictos, quia non est superius, transit auctor ad potentiam que consequitur ad omnia: non enim est res naturali potentia carens, que in suo actu naturali naturaliter se habente, per quem manifestatur potentia et ideo est lumen potentie, melius est quam in se nude considerata. Potentie vero viventes, ut sunt potentie anime vegetative, et magis viventes, que sunt anime sensitive, et adhuc magis, que sunt anime rationalis, meliores sunt potentiis naturalibus corporum et hiis omnibus sunt potentie meliores que sunt substantie, ut potentie angelice: omnes enim celestes substantie angelice communiter dicuntur celestes virtutes, hoc est celestes potentie: nomen enim Grecum quod hic ponitur pro "potentia" et in Ierarchia Angelica pro "virtutes celestes," quod etiam aliqui[13] transtulerunt hic in virtutem, idem est nomen, scilicet *dynamis*. Hec itaque abnegans auctor per ordinem a causa omnium, adiungit: *neque habet potentiam, neque potentia est*, que melior est habente potentiam; *neque lumen*, id est neque potentia agens, manifestata et declarata per actum; *neque vivit*, ut potentie anime; *neque vita* est, que melior est vivente; *neque substantia est*, ut sunt potentie et

---

[11] Cf. Augustine, *De civitate Dei*, XIX, 13.
[12] Cf. ibid.: "pax omnium rerum tranquillitas ordinis."
[13] Hilduin, Eriugena and Sarrazen.

all things, and saying: *it is not number*. And because order follows immediately upon number, order which confers good on both number and the things to which number applies (for without order there is only chaos and disturbance), he immediately adds: *nor order*; and since order is an arrangement that gives its place to each one of several things that are themselves equal and unequal to each other, in order there necessarily is the greater (in whatever mode of priority belongs to the prior things,) the lesser (in whatever way of derivativeness belongs to the later things,) and equality (of the things that are equal). Through that there necessarily is similitude and dissimilitude. All these belong to the perfection and the goodness of order. And so he goes on, immediately denying these things of the cause of all, and says: *it is not greatness*, so called from being greater through priority in the order; *nor smallness*, so called from being the lesser state of coming later in the order; *nor equality*, in the order of things that are equal, *nor similarity* of equal things *nor dissimilarity* of things unequal; for the cause of all things is none of these.

And since beyond the order of things there is no place where the ascent can be taken further (for order brings all things into peace), the author returns to motion and rest, which follow on disjunctively to all things, denying each of these with regard to the cause of all things. But rest, opposite to the motion that follows on to all, he divides into station (which is the privation of action), and sensible motion and silence (which is the privation of intelligible action and motion). For intelligible things act only by means of an intelligible word. Therefore, denying both (that is, rest and motion) with regard to the cause of all, he says, *it neither stays at rest nor is it moved, nor does it bring about silence*. But since beyond rest and motion thus generally intended there is no higher thing, the author passes on to the power which belongs to all things. For there is nothing that lacks natural power, which is manifested in its own natural act in its natural state; and therefore the light of potency is better than potency considered purely in itself. Indeed the living powers, such as the powers of the vegetative soul, and the more living which belong to the sensitive soul, and the more living still which belong to the rational soul, are better than the natural powers of bodies. Better than all of these are the powers which are substances, such as the angelic powers. Now all the celestial, angelic substances are called in common "celestial virtues," that is, celestial powers; the Greek noun which is employed here for potency and in the *Angelic Hierarchy* for celestial virtues (which some have also translated here by *virtus* ["virtue"]) is the same, namely *dynamis*. And so, negating these things one by one of the cause of all, the author adds: *It does not have power nor is it power*, which is better than what has potency; *nor light*, that is, not an active power manifested and clarified through act; *nor does it live* like the powers of the soul, *nor is it life*, because it is better than what lives; *it is not substance*, as are the angelic, celestial powers and virtues. Above these there is no power higher or closer to God, and therefore the author returns to the measure which follows upon the being

virtutes angelice celestes. Supra quas non est potentia sublimior aut Deo propinquior, et ideo redit auctor ad mensuram que consequitur ad esse omnis exsistentis, abnegans eam a causa prima; que mensura dividitur, ut supra dictum est in libro De Divinis Nominibus, in seculum et tempus, et seculum est excellentior mensura quam tempus; unde sequitur: *neque seculum, neque tempus est*, videlicet prima causa. Sed si seculum est melius et Deo propinquius quam tempus, et hic ascendit a distantioribus ad propinquiora, debuit sic ordinasse suum sermonem ut temporis abnegatio precederet. Ad quod dici potest quod non intendebat hec divisim abnegare, sed per hoc coniunctim simpliciter mensuram existendi, vel quia, ut in dicto libro predictum est, seculum quandoque sumitur pro tempore et tempus pro seculo et dicitur tempus seculare et seculum temporale, in huius insinuationem preposuit auctor seculum et postposuit tempus, relinquens tempori superioris significationem.

Supra mensuram vero communiter continentem seculum et tempus, non est mensura Deo et eternitati propinquior, et ideo transit auctor ad naturalem appetitum naturaliter omnibus insitum qui, quia est simpliciter boni, nobilior est et melior aliis pretactis communiter ad omnia consequentibus. Hic autem appetitus, quanto est in naturis superioribus et nobilioribus, tanto melior est et Deo propinquior, unde in naturis et potentiis apprehensivis, que quandoque comprehenduntur sub scientia, melior est quam in carentibus apprehensione, et in apprehensivo superiori melior quam in inferiori, et in apprehensivo non errante circa apprehensum melior quam in errante, et in apprehensivo non errante circa apprehensum, qui habet potestatem imperativam agendorum, melior eo qui caret potestativo imperio, et qui habet potestatem imperativam non errans in actibus, melior eo qui in actibus errat. Optimus igitur est appetitus boni sciens non errans in actu sciendi, imperativus agendorum nec errans in agendo, et hic est omnium maxime in se unitus et appropinquans unitati supersimplici, unde dici potest et unum et unitas. Naturalem itaque omnibus insitum appetitum boni, secundum hos dictos ascensus ad optimum, abnegans auctor a causa omnium, subiungit: *neque tactus intelligibilis*, id est appetitus naturalis *est ipsius* cause videlicet omnium, *neque scientia est*, id est apprehensio per quam sit vel habeat appetitum apprehensivum, *neque veritas est*, id est privatio erroris circa apprehensum, *neque regnum*, id est potestas imperativa agendorum; *neque sapientia*, id est privatio erroris in agendo, que maxime est sapientia, ut per hec videlicet simul iuncta, sit appetitus optimus et rerum optima; *neque unum, neque unitas* per dictam videlicet optimitatem in se maxime unitum, et maxima proximitas ad supersimplicem unitatem.

of every existent, denying this of the first cause. This measure is divided (as was said above in the book *On Divine Names*) into everlastingness and time; everlastingness is a more excellent measure than time, whence it follows: *not everlastingness nor time* (meaning: the first cause). But if everlastingness is better and closer to God than time, and [the author] is ascending from the more distant things to the nearer things, he should have gone about the ordering of his discourse in such a way that the negation of time would have had priority. It could be said [in reply] to that, that he was intending here not to negate these [two concepts] disjunctively, but by simply taking the two terms together [to negate] the measure of existing; or that (as has already been said in the book referred to) everlastingness sometimes is taken for time and time sometimes for everlastingness, and you can speak of an everlasting time and a temporal lastingness. To suggest this the author has put first everlastingness and then time, leaving to time the reference to what is higher.

However, above the measure which commonly contains everlastingness and time there is no measure closer to God and to eternity. Therefore the author passes on to the natural appetite which is naturally innate in all things, which, since it is simply for the good, is nobler and better than all other things referred to which commonly belong to all things. This appetite, however, is better and closer to God to the extent that it is in higher and more noble natures. And so, in the natures and powers relative to knowing which are sometimes understood under the nature of knowledge, this [appetite] is better than in things which lack knowledge, and in the higher knowing power it is better than in the lower; and in the knowing power that does not err concerning its object it is better than in something which does err; and in the power of knowing which does not err concerning its object and which has the power to command action, it is better than in that which lacks that power of command. The one which has the power to command and does not err in its acts is better than the one which does err in its acts. The best, therefore, is the appetite of the good that knows, and does not err in the act of knowledge, that commands the actions and does not err in acting. Of all things this is the most united in itself. It comes close to that super-simple unity, and on that account it can be called both one and unity. So, denying of the cause of all things that natural appetite for the good which is innate in all (denying it according to the order of the ways of ascent towards the very best that we have outlined,) the author adds: *no understanding* (that is, the natural appetite) *grasps it,* (meaning: the cause of all things); *it is not knowledge,* that is, the apprehension through which it may be or may have the desire for knowing, *nor truth,* that is, the privation of error concerning what it knows; *nor kingship,* that is, the power commanding the things to be done; *nor wisdom,* that is, the privation of error in acting, which is wisdom in the highest sense of the word; in such a way that through all these things joined together [the Cause] would be the best appetite and the best of things. *It is neither one nor unity* (meaning: through the aforesaid best

Isti itaque sunt ascensus per rerum omnium ab infimis per media usqua ad summa abnegationes, nec in hiis ponit metam ascensions ingressurus in caliginem, sed ascendens superius abnegat a Deo quicquid potest vis cognoscitiva creata per nominationes quascumque positivas de ipso comprehendere vel cognoscere. Unde sequitur: *neque deitas est*, videlicet omnium causa, *vel bonitas*, et similiter intellige de ceteris nominibus de tota Trinitate dictis, et similiter de discretive dictis de personis, unde sequitur: *neque spiritus est, ut nos scire*, id est ut contingit nos scire et intelligere spiritum, *neque filiatio neque paternitas*. Ultra hec non restat abdicabile ab omnium causa specialiter: ingressurus tamen in caliginem post dictas abnegationes colligens generaliter, dicit; *neque aliud quid est*, videlicet omnium causa, *cognitorum nobis*, hominibus videlicet, *vel alii alicui entium*, utpote angelo, *neque quid non entium neque quid entium est*; ita, inquam, ascendentes usque ad caliginem, dicamus quod neque anima est neque cetera que predicta sunt usque huc. Et iam quasi ingredientes vel ingressi caliginem, dicamus hoc advertentes et solum cognoscentes quod *neque entia noscunt ipsam*, omnium videlicet causam, *secundum quod ipsa est, neque ipsa cognoscit entia secundum quod entia sunt*, non enim habet virtutes aliquas cognoscitivas suscipientes quid a cognitis, sed supercognoscitivam, quia supersubstantialiter cognoscens se, cognoscit omnia; *neque ratio* seu sermo *ipsius est, neque nomen, neque cognitio*; non enim attingit ad ipsam causam omnium, secundum quod ipsa est in se, aliqua cognitio vel nominatio; *neque tenebra est*, id est luminis privatio, *neque lumen*, visibile videlicet, ut est in se, ab aliqua virtute spiritaliter visiva, propter sui superexcessum et inaccessibilitatem; *neque error* per deviationem a veritate; *neque veritas*, ad quam videlicet comprehendendam vis cognoscitiva potest attingere; *neque universaliter est ipsius positio neque ablatio, sed facientes positiones et ablationes*, de ipsa videlicet, *eorum que post ipsam, neque ponimus ipsam, neque auferimus, quia et super omnem positionem est omnino perfecta et unitiva omnium causa, et superxcellentia absoluti simpliciter ab omnibus et ultra universa*, seu tota est, resume, super omnem ablationem.

Cum mens itaque superexcesserit omnia et abnegaverit omnia tam specialiter quam generaliter ab omnium causa, et quieverit a comprehensione omnium, absorpta tota in desiderium ipsius, et superexcellentia luminis ipsius inaccessibilitatis ei incognite eluxerit in ipsa inaccessibilitate et inaccessibilitatis caligine, incognite cognoscit quod ipsam omnium causam secundum quod est in se, nihil potest cognoscere, et quod ipsa nullo indiget extra se et sui simplicitatem ut quicquam cognoscat, et in hoc incognite cognoscit

nature, the one that is maximally united in itself, the maximal proximity to that more-than-simple unity.)

And so these are the ascents through the negations of all things, from the lowest through the intermediary right up to the highest. In these the one who is to enter the darkness does not make any delay, but going higher he negates of God whatever the created power of knowledge can comprehend or know concerning him, through whatever positive namings you like. Whence there follows: *nor is it deity* (meaning: the cause of all things) *or goodness*. Similarly apply that understanding to the other names given to the whole Trinity, and in the same way to the things said individually concerning the persons. So there follows: *It is not Spirit in the sense that we understand that*, that is, as we happen to know and to understand the Spirit, *nor sonship nor fatherhood*. Beyond these there remains no predication which can be removed from the cause of all by some special term. However, the one who is to enter the darkness collects all these negations together and says: *Nor is it anything else*, meaning: the cause of all, *of the things known to us*, that is, to men *or to any other being* such as an angel. *Nor is it anything among non-existents or among existents*. And so, I say, let us ascend right up to the darkness and say that he is neither soul nor the other things that have been mentioned up to now. And now as though entering or having entered the darkness let us say this, noticing, and only knowing, that *existents do not know it* (the cause of all) *as it itself is, nor does it know existing things as such*. For he does not have some powers of knowledge receiving something from objects known, but rather he has a power of knowing that is beyond that, since by knowing himself in a way that is beyond being, he knows all things. *There is no expression* or discourse *of it, nor name nor knowledge*, for there is no knowledge or naming which reaches the cause of all things in what it is in itself. *It is not darkness*, that is, the privation of light, and *it is not light*, meaning: [not] visible as it is in itself by any power of spiritual vision, because of its transcendence of itself and inaccessibility. *It is not error* through deviation from the truth, *nor truth*, meaning by that a power of knowledge which can get to understanding. *It is completely beyond any assertion or any taking away; when we make assertions or take away* [attributes] concerning it *coming from those things that come after it we neither assert nor remove anything concerning it, since beyond every assertion it is the perfect and uniting cause of all things, and it transcends all taking away by virtue of its simple and absolute nature beyond all things*, or it is whole, I mean above all negation.

And so, when the mind shall have transcended all things and negated all, both specially and generally, regarding the cause of all, and when it shall have rested from the comprehension of all, absorbed completely in the desire of it; and the transcendent light of its inaccessibility shall have shone on it in an unknowing way, in that very inaccessibility itself and in the darkness of inaccessibility, unknowingly the mind knows that it can know nothing of that self-same cause of all, taken in what it is in itself, and that

quod nulla vis ad ipsam et in ipsam potest, et quod ipsa non est quicquam deficiens vel sufficiens, et universaliter quod neque est aliquid neque nihil; incognite enim cognoscit quod est super et ante aliquid et super et ante nihil. Quod autem nulla vis simpliciter in ipsam potest, insinuat auctor per hoc quod nec ratio nec vis nominum positiva nec cognoscitiva, que vires in plus possunt quam vis altera, in ipsam non possunt. Per lumen vero et veritatem, que sunt res summe, insinuat omnem rem non deficientem, et per tenebram et errorem rem omnem deficientem.

Isti itaque, quos pro modulo nostro exposuimus, sunt ascensus in caliginem, secundum quam superlucidam oramus cum auctore nos et omnes fieri, et horum a nobis de superexcellenti negotio deficienter nimirum dictorum defectus a perfectis benivole supleri.

the latter needs nothing outside of itself and of its simplicity in order to know a thing. In this [the mind] unknowingly knows that no power can reach it and into it, and that [the cause] is not something deficient or sufficient; and in the widest terms, that it is neither something nor nothing. For unknowingly the mind knows that it is above and before anything, and above and before nothing. But the author suggests that no power can simply attain it, in that neither reason nor the positive force of names nor the power of knowing (powers which are capable of more than any other power) are of any value with regard to it. By light and truth, however, which are the highest things, he suggests everything that is not deficient, and through darkness and error everything that is deficient.

These, then, which we have expounded insofar as our limitations allow, are the ascents into the darkness, in which more-than-bright darkness we pray, with the author, that we and all may come to be; and we ask the perfect to supply with goodwill what is lacking in what we have said concerning this transcendent treatise.

CONCLUSION

Thomas Gallus and Robert Grosseteste, Scholars and Friends

Linked through Adam Marsh, O.F.M.

The two commentators whose work we have presented were linked not only by shared intellectual and religious interests but through personal acquaintance and friendship, and even the exchange of their writings. So much is clear from a letter addressed by Adam Marsh, O.F.M., the collaborator and intimate friend of Grosseteste, to Thomas Gallus at Vercelli.[1] Marsh spoke to his correspondent of the bishop as being *amantis-simus vester Dominus Lincolniae* — "your most dear friend." The letter was written in 1241–1242. It emerges from it that Adam sent Gallus a copy of a commentary on the *Angelic Hierarchy*, which can only have been Grosseteste's work. Adam in turn had a request to make: could he please have the comment on MT which Thomas had "recently" finished (this must be the *Explanacio* on the MT, of ca. 1241), and also his commentary on *Divine Names* "when he has it done" (it was in fact completed on April 27, 1242)? Marsh evidently knew Gallus quite well. The presence of the latter in England during the early months of 1238 (to visit the church at Chesterton which had been granted to the Abbey of Vercelli) would have allowed the three men to meet. The letter of Marsh makes it likely that Grosseteste had access to some of Gallus's work as he was writing his own commentaries on the Pseudo-Dionysius. Marsh seems to have known the *Extractio* of Gallus (1238), and the *Explanacio* on the MT may conceivably have been on Grosseteste's desk as he composed his own. It is not likely, on the other hand, that Thomas would have brought his friend in 1238 the glosses or *Expositio* which he had finalized in 1232, since he would have regarded the *Extractio* as having surpassed his earlier effort. We must conclude that either Grosseteste had read the *Expositio* before 1238 or else (which seems more likely) he did not have any acquaintance with it.

---

[1] See Callus, "The Date of Grosseteste's …," pp. 189–194.

Similarities of Approach as Interpreters

In their approach to MT the glosses of Thomas Gallus and the commentary of Robert Grosseteste resemble each other in more ways than one. Both scholastics had regard to the corpus consisting of all four writings as the only proper context for the interpretation of MT. This wholesome hermeneutic contrasts with the frequent isolation in which MT was to be copied and studied (along with glosses and commentaries) during the later Middle Ages. The approach of Gallus and Grosseteste had as its consequence that kataphatic and apophatic theology were held in truly dialectical tension, in the best Neoplatonic tradition, and not allowed to fall apart. A negation, if it is to have any meaning and reference, must be (and must remain) parasitic upon an affirmation, one which is not removed or destroyed by its opposite but rather opened up to the infinite. Both Gallus and Grosseteste had a firm grasp of this truth and sought to pass it on to their readers. Grosseteste's ordering of the four works, placing MT at the end, may have had the effect of emphasizing the dialectical unity of kataphatic and apophatic discourses, as he pointed out the affirmative nature of the first three treatises and the negative theological character of the fourth.

It may be recalled that Gallus developed the affective dimension of the highest contact between God and the soul: where conceptual thought must be surpassed in the movement of the soul to God, the attraction of love fills the vacuum and supplies a new "knowledge," coming from direct acquaintance and being beyond thought and speech. The reader of Grosseteste's commentary can verify the presence in it of a similar thought. Perhaps the influence of Thomas upon Robert lies in this "affective Dionysianism" more than in anything else.

The shared Augustinian heritage can also be uncovered in the conviction that the vision of God is experienced by the angels and the blessed without the mediation of "theophanies" of the kind which Pseudo-Dionysius and Eriugena had spoken of: it is a vision "face to face" (I Cor 13:12). This conviction affected the theory of mystical experience which Gallus and Grosseteste rallied to: the union between God and the soul is not mediated by any creaturely influence, any more than is the vision of the blessed. In this regard both scholars were quite consciously following the line laid down by Hugh of St. Victor in his interpretation of the *Celestial Hierarchy*. Grosseteste's friendship with Gallus, his affinity with his thought, and even his deep interest in the Pseudo-Dionysian corpus and its Latinization, may, I suggest, be regarded as markers that relate him directly to the School of St. Victor at Paris.

Difference in Hermeneutical Approach

Our two commentators came, broadly speaking, to similar conclusions in mystical theory. However, they approached the text of MT somewhat differently — Gallus as a conscious facilitator of a resolutely monoglot, Latin readership, and Grosseteste as a serious philologist. Thomas inherited the ambition of John Sarrazen, which was to improve on the literalism, the obscurity (for the Latin reader) and the translating blunders of the version by Eriugena. Sarrazen might even be thought of, ironically, as the translator of Eriugena — into Latin! — for that may well be how he saw his role: to produce a more readable and flowing version of the *Corpus Dionysiacum*. Gallus in turn attempted to take this aim further along the same course by improving upon the readability of Sarrazen's version — and then improving upon his own improvements! The huge success which awaited his efforts showed just how well he had judged the requirements of the scholastic milieu at Paris.

Grosseteste, on the other hand (as we have indicated in introducing his work on MT), applied all his Greek knowledge and his late-acquired Hellenist and Byzantinist culture to the exegesis of the meaning, which is to say, of the words, of the Pseudo-Dionysius. Words, words, words! — that was his whole business as exegete. He made no concessions to those who wanted a quick digest (or "extract") which they could assimilate with some ease. Grosseteste expressed his determination to disregard any aim at readable Latin in his translation and commentary, in favor of a serious, and inevitably quaint and foreign-sounding, exploration of the vocabulary, the thought-structures and the spiritual message of the Pseudo-Areopagite. He did not spare himself nor his team (for he had helpers), but his work was too lengthy and too philological to attract any but serious scholars to copy and use it.[2] Gallus's was a good example of the successful *assimilation* of a foreign-language work, whereas Grosseteste wanted his Latin reader to achieve a truly hermeneutical *sense of the difference* between Latin and Greek as languages and vehicles of culture, even within the Christian unity.

Friends Circulating Together

The convergence between the interpretations of MT by Thomas Gallus and Robert Grosseteste, and the complementary nature of their interpretations, attracted the attention of a number of medieval scholars, who individually set scribes to work copying

---

[2] For Grosseteste's method as translator and exegete see James McEvoy, *The Philosophy of Robert Grosseteste*, 2nd ed. (Oxford: Oxford University Press, 1986), part I, chap. 2.

alternating extracts from the *Exposicio* and the *Commentarius*. Six manuscripts, all of South German and Austrian provenance, conform to this description. To these may be added the Strasbourg printing of 1502–1503, which contained the version and commentary of *Lincolniensis* and also the Sarrazen translation together with the *Extractio* of *Vercellensis* on MT. The material link thus forged by later centuries between their interpretations corresponded quite happily to a historical reality, for together these two friends may be said to have initiated the second Latin reception of the *Mystical Theology*. Their individual efforts united to launch what rapidly became a movement.

It cannot be too much emphasized that the entire later interpretation of MT was deflected into the path it actually followed through the combined influence of Thomas Gallus and Robert Grosseteste. These earliest Latin commentators provided the context within which not only the mystical theology of monastery and university but also the actual spiritual experience of countless souls was to be formed. MT may justly be described as the most influential treatise in late medieval spirituality. However, the spirituality it conveyed was not, or was not only, the dialectical ascent through knowing and unknowing that is the true meaning of the Greek work (that culmination of the Areopagite's message), but the transconceptual ecstasy of the individual soul that passes through purification and illumination to union with God, by means of an exceptional grace of divine love. The centrality of love, and of Jesus Christ, in Western mystical doctrine and practice had no counterpart in MT, where the former was not so much as mentioned. It is scarcely thinkable that the book as it stands would have entered into the mainstream of medieval spirituality had not its first commentators ventured a full-scale reappropriation of its contents. The following passage from a conference pronounced by Bishop Grosseteste encapsulates the added value which he brought to MT, likely enough under the influence of Gallus:

> Since after this ascent love has no further place to seek and find the Beloved through its own vehemence, drawing back all the lower powers mentioned and making them rest from all their acts, it apprehends nothing at all, but stands beyond all creatures and beyond itself in the darkness of the actual unknowing both of itself and of all things, waiting like Moses on the dark summit of the mountain for the Beloved to manifest himself to it directly. Only when this has occurred does the noblest power of the soul enjoy full life.[3]

"Mystical theology" can be rendered "hidden speech of God," in other words, apophatic theology. The harmonization between the book of that name (MT) and the biblical Canticle of love is the meaning of the thought quoted above. In this passage the crucial dimension of mysticism (in the distinctively modern sense of the term) is already

---

[3] Grosseteste, *Ecclesia sancta celebrat*, ¶ 36, pp. 186–87 (ed. McEvoy, 1980). This passage runs closely parallel to his comment on MT I.1.

present. The words of Grosseteste look forward to St. Bonaventure, *The Cloud of Unknowing*, Chancellor Gerson, and perhaps also in some measure to the women mystics who were drawn, not to the apophatic treatise and the questions and discussions which it raised, but beyond theology to Jesus Christ as their Beloved.

TRIPARTITE BIBLIOGRAPHY

1. THOMAS GALLUS

Johannis Scoti Expositiones seu Glossae in Mysticam Theologiam S. Dionysii, PL 122, cols. 267–284.

Gabriel Théry, O.P., "L'inauthenticité du commentaire de la *Théologie mystique* attribué à Jean Scot Érigène," *Vie spirituelle* 8 (1923), Supplément, pp. 137–57.

Thomas Gallus. Grand commentaire sur la Théologie mystique, ed. Gabriel Théry, O.P. (Paris: Haloua, 1934).

Jean Châtillon, "De Guillaume de Champeaux à Thomas Gallus. Chronique d'histoire littéraire et doctrinale de l'École de Saint-Victor," *Revue du moyen-âge latin* 8 (1952), pp. 139–264.

Manuel Alonso, S.J., *Pedro Hispano, Exposição sobre os livros Beato Dionisio Areopagita* (Lisbon: Centro de Estudos de Psicologia e de Historia de Filosofia, 1957).

J. Walsh, "The 'Expositions' of Thomas Gallus on the Pseudo-Dionysian Letters," *Archives d'histoire doctrinale et littéraire du moyen âge* 30 (1963), pp. 199–220.

M. Capellino, *Tommaso di San Vittore abate vercellese* (Vercelli: Biblioteca della Società Storica Vercellese, 1978).

Martin Grabmann, "Ein dem Petrus Hispanus zugeschriebener Kommentar zu den Schriften des Pseudo-Areopagiten," in idem, *Gesammelte Akademieabhandlungen*, Veröffentlichungen des Grabmann-Instituts, N.F. 25/2 (Paderborn/Munich: Schöningh, 1979), pp. 1238–46.

Jeanne Barbet, "Thomas Gallus," in *Dictionnaire de spiritualité ascétique et mystique*, vol. 15 (1991), cols. 800–16.

Bernard McGinn, *The Flowering of Mysticism* (New York: Crossroad, 1998).

Marshall E. Crossnoe, "Education and the Care of Souls: Pope Gregory IX, the Order of St. Victor and the University of Paris in 1237," *Mediaeval Studies* 61 (1999), pp. 137–72.

James McEvoy, "Thomas Gallus (Abbas Vercellensis) and the Commentary on the *De Mystica Theologia* ascribed to Iohannes Scottus Eriugena. With a Concluding Note on the Second Latin Reception of the Pseudo-Dionysius (1230–1250)," in *Traditions of Platonism: Essays in Honour of John Dillon*, ed. J. J. Cleary (Aldershot, Hampshire: Ashgate, 1999), pp. 389–405.

James McEvoy, "John Scottus Eriugena and Thomas Gallus, Commentators on the *Mystical Theology*," in *History and Eschatology in Eriugena and His Time*, ed. J. McEvoy and M. Dunne, Ancient and Medieval Philosophy, Series 1, 30 (Louvain: Leuven University Press, 2002), pp. 183–202.

2. ROBERT GROSSETESTE

Ulderico Gamba, "Commenti latini al *De mystica theologia* del pseudo-Dionigi Areopagita fino al Grossatesta," *Aevum* 16 (1942), pp. 251–71.

Ulderico Gamba, *Il commento di Roberto Grossatesta al "De Mystica Theologia" del pseudo-Dionigi l'Areopagita* (Milan: Vita e Pensiero, 1942), v+69 pp.

François Ruello, "Un commentaire dionysien en quête d'auteur," *Archives d'histoire doctrinale et littéraire du moyen âge* 22 (1953), pp. 141–81.

James McEvoy, "Robert Grosseteste's Theory of Human Nature. With the Text of his Conference *Ecclesia Sancta Celebrat*," *Recherches de théologie ancienne et médiévale* 47 (1980), pp. 131–87. (Reprinted in James McEvoy, *Robert Grosseteste: Exegete and Philosopher* [Aldershot, Hampshire: Ashgate, 1994].)

A. C. Dionisotti, "On the Greek Studies of Robert Grosseteste," in *The Uses of Greek and Latin: Historical Essays*, ed. A. C. Dionisotti, A. Grafton, and J. Kraye (London: Warburg Institute, 1988), pp. 19–39.

Deirdre Carabine, "Robert Grosseteste's Commentary on the *Mystical Theology* of Pseudo-Dionysius," in *Robert Grosseteste: New Perspectives on His Thought and Scholarship*, ed. James McEvoy, Instrumenta Patristica 27 (Turnhout: Brepols, 1995), pp. 169–87.

3. GALLUS AND GROSSETESTE

The Works of Dionysius the Areopagite, trans. Rev. John Parker (London: Parker & Co., 1897), *Mystic Theology*, pp. 130–37.

Dionysiaca, ed. U. Chevallier, 2 vols. (Bruges/Paris: Desclée, 1937).

Daniel A. Callus, O.P., "The Date of Grosseteste's Translations and Commentaries on Pseudo-Dionysius and the *Nichomachean Ethics*," *Recherches de théologie ancienne et médiévale* 14 (1947), pp. 186–209.

The Complete Works of Pseudo-Dionysius, trans. Colm Luibheid, The Classics of Western Spirituality (New York: Paulist Press, 1987), pp. 133–42.

Kurt Ruh, *Geschichte der abendländischen Mystik*, vol. 3: *Die Mystik des deutschen Predigerordens und ihre Grundlegung durch die Hochscholastik* (Munich: Beck, 1996).

Deirdre Carabine, *John Scottus Eriugena*, Great Medieval Thinkers (New York, Oxford University Press, 2000), pp. 58–66.

INDEX

Index

I. MANUSCRIPTS

II. SCRIPTURAL REFERENCES